How to
TRACK and
FIND GAME

AN OUTDOOR LIFE BOOK

How to
TRACK and
FIND GAME

Clyde Ormond

Illustrated by
Douglas Allen Jr.

OUTDOOR LIFE • FUNK & WAGNALLS
New York

Library of Congress Catalog Card Number: 74-33565
Funk & Wagnalls Hardcover Edition: ISBN 0-308-10210-X
Paperback Edition: ISBN 0-308-10211-8

Designed by Jeff Fitschen

Manufactured in the United States of America

Contents

Introduction

WHENEVER WILD GAME ANIMALS move over the land they leave a record in the form of spoor. Some of the evidence of their passing, such as animal scent and tracks, is temporary in nature. The elements of storm, weather, and season gradually dissipate it until it virtually disappears.

Other forms of spoor, such as dung, hairs left on foliage or the ground as the animal passes, and deciduous antlers shed annually by the males of some species endure longer. Such spoor as the deep trails left by the passing of many animals may last for years and become something of a permanent record of the species.

The novice outdoorsman, upon seeing a sample of wild animal spoor such as a plain track in the dirt, is apt to conclude simply that some kind of animal has passed that way. A veteran outdoorsman who has become skilled in reading wildlife sign, however, may well be able to tell much more from the same track. He can identify the animal, whether it be deer, elk, moose, bear, or some other creature. He can tell with a fair degree of accuracy whether the animal is alone or in the company of others of its species; whether it is male or female; if it is frightened, feeding, or leisurely passing through. More important to the locating of game, he can study the track, correlate it with the surrounding country, and tell where that particular animal is likely to be at the moment.

Reading wild animal sign, coupled with the ability to find such game in relation to its habitat and field behavior, is a real art. Like any other art, it must be learned from study, observation, and practice.

For generations hunters have made the greatest use of the ability to track and locate game. In fact these skills and techniques have enabled many a people to survive. They are still as applicable today when hunting is a sport and recreation rather than a means of procuring meat. Indeed, with today's hunting pressure and dwindling game herds, the need for locating game remains great. It is a known fact among most hunters that those who have cultivated this skill are the most successful at the sport.

1

There are other forms of outdoor activity where skill in locating and stalking wild animals is vital. The outdoor-wildlife photographer (and this includes any outdoorsman who likes to take pictures of the wildlife he comes upon) has an even greater need of this skill than the hunter. This is simply because his camera lens does not function adequately at the long ranges that the hunting rifle can cover.

Any outdoorsman will find that an ability to read animal sign, to locate the game within the area he travels, and to stalk it to within a range where he can observe it and enjoy it, will greatly add to his love for the outdoors. He will learn, as he locates and studies the animals, that he is witnessing an ecology and life pattern comparable to his own. There is the same struggle for food, for survival, for mates, and for safety and a better existence.

PART ONE

BIG GAME

1

Mule Deer

THE MULE DEER *(Odocoileus hemionus hemionus)* is one of North America's most noble and prized big-game animals. It inhabits the western half of the United States and adjacent areas in Mexico and Canada. Regions of large mule-deer concentrations include the Kaibab Forest in Arizona, the Jicarilla Indian Reservation in New Mexico, and the Middle Fork of the Salmon River country in central Idaho. Mule deer love the broken hill country of the West, ranging above timberline in summer, migrating downward in winter to the open sagebrush flats.

A buck mule deer weighs up to 300 pounds; the doe goes up to 180 pounds. Both sexes are gray in fall and winter, blending with the drab coloration of winter vegetation; their reddish summer coat blends well with the flowers and greenery of the season. The bucks have large bifurcated antlers, and both sexes have huge mulelike ears and puny, ropelike tails.

The track of a big mule-deer buck is heart shaped. The imprints left by the front hoofs are a trifle blunter and larger than those of the hind feet. The tracks of an exceptional buck measure about 3 inches, the doe's somewhat less.

The dung of mule deer is generally segmented, the kernels being about ½ inch in diameter and the shape of hazelnuts. Dung in piles means the animal was standing and unalerted, whereas droppings strung out indicate that it was moving and possibly alerted.

In learning to track and locate mule deer, the beginner should not be misled by the numerous tracks left in canyon bottoms and creek beds. This animal, like many other species, ranges high within its habitat during daylight hours but comes down to drink at creeks during the night. This is a safety strategy that is instinctive to the animal. It knows that danger normally comes from below, and that darkness will conceal it from its enemies, including man. So it descends at dusk to feed and drink, and with approaching daylight ascends to the higher elevations, knowing that enemies will follow from below. There is, however, a subtler safety strategy at

5

By day, mule deer favor mountain ridges that afford escape routes, favorable visibility, and scent-carrying thermal currents.

Fore

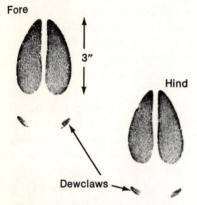

3"

Hind

Dewclaws →

The front hoof is slightly blunter than the hind and may measure up to 3 inches. Dewclaws of all types of deer register in soft terrain, as shown here, or when the animal runs, as illustrated in the next chapter.

Mule deer droppings are generally segmented kernels about ½ inch in diameter.

work here. Since cool air descends and warm air rises, by ascending with warm air at sunup, the deer moves within a narrow belt of air that contains its own scent.

Tracking a mule deer is difficult, both on bare ground and in snow. One may unravel the tracks and locate the game, but in doing so he will more often than not reveal his own presence and the game will flee. For the mule deer, like other species, constantly watches its backtrack to detect approaching enemies. Moreover, it plans that backtrack so as to compel any enemy in pursuit to reveal his presence.

For instance, a buck may leave tracks in fresh snow as he heads up a canyon. As he travels the buck will periodically move from one side of the canyon to the other, turning to watch his backtrack. At some point in his travels, the buck purposely crosses an opening in the timber or vegetation through which a tracker (man or predator) must pass, and through which the buck, in his backtracking, could observe.

The experienced hunter, instead of doggedly pursuing the trail, interprets the tracks, dung, and other spoor and then proceeds to locate the game according to his own plan, not the buck's.

If the spoor is fresh, the animal is not too far away. If the track is large, single in pattern, and meandering, with a pace length of approximately 18 inches, the implications are that the buck is alone, feeding occasionally, and not alerted. It is probably headed upward after a night's drink at the creek and will be somewhere up in the canyon or on one of its ridges.

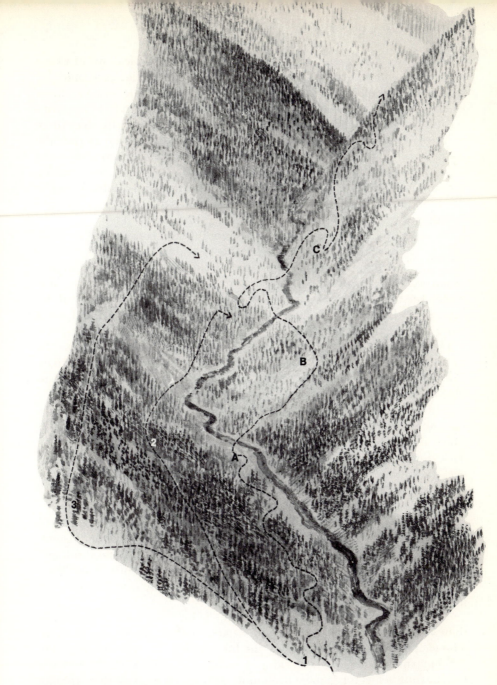

Lone-hunter strategy. Meandering tracks about 18 inches apart indicate that the mule deer is feeding and is not yet alerted. Along its route, the animal will purposely cross clearings and then watch its backtrack for pursuing enemies. In the above drawing, if the hunter (1) were to follow closely upon the tracks in the snow, the deer might see him pass through clearings A, B, or C. The hunter has two better options: He can roughly parallel the deer's trail along the left slope (2). Or, since the deer may already be watching, the hunter can pretend to depart and then move along the ridge (3), scanning likely areas.

The hunter then heads after the animal, not from indications of where it has been, but according to where its field behavior indicates it might be. The basic rule for hunting mule deer is to concentrate on the ridges where, in the fall, the deer are most frequently to be found. The reasons for this predilection are many. First, the ridges always afford the deer three avenues of escape—either side down the mountainside, and back over the route already traveled. Moreover, the sparse vegetation there makes for easier movement. Especially in early morning, the deer find their food on the sunny slopes just off such ridges. At midday they can shade up and lie down on the northern slopes of the ridges, where the heavier timber and foliage protect them from their enemies.

The hunter then, trying to find his game, should concentrate on these ridges, where abundant spoor gives the best evidence of the game's location. The technique is simple. The hunter climbs a high ridge in known or suspected deer country. He looks for spoor in the partially bare game trails that he knows mule deer will favor. He hunts from daybreak till sunup and from dusk to dark, since mule deer are nocturnal and move more at these times.

The places to watch during these periods are the openings on the sunny side of the ridges and the lower slopes where the sun strikes. The wise hunter moves slowly, keeping himself concealed as much as possible by staying just inside the fringing vegetation as he climbs the hill.

If no game is found as he ascends one ridge, he then works around the canyon, or gully end, watching not only the slopes but also the saddle over which mule deer normally cross into the next canyon or gully, and then back down on the spine of the next ridge. Since mule deer watch their backtrack and expect danger from below, hunting the second ridge downward may be just as productive as hunting the first ridge upward. Mule deer are less suspicious of pursuit from above.

For midday approaching of mule deer, one must be doubly careful to stalk quietly and unseen. The game then is shaded up in heavier vegetation, and the breaking of twigs or swishing of brush against one's pant legs is sure to give one away. More often than not in this kind of midday hunting one jumps the game—that is, suddenly spooks it, so that it takes off in great bounds.

Another fine way of hunting mule deer is on horseback. This can be done for itself, or while locating other game such as elk, moose, or bear. The technique is much the same—the hunter rides up the high ridges in early morning, watching both sides of each ridge and constantly studying the canyons below for game. Often mule deer spook less from a horseman than from somebody moving about on foot.

2

Whitetail Deer

THE WHITETAIL DEER *(Odocoileus virginianus)* might well be called the all-American deer. It inhabits all the contiguous forty-eight states with the exception of about a half-dozen that form a thin strip extending from California eastward to Ohio. States with the largest population include Michigan, Wisconsin, Pennsylvania, Minnesota, Texas, and New York. The fact that the whitetail abounds in these heavily urban states indicates that it can live well in close proximity to man. It also has the capacity to survive in the more arid brushlands.

In most areas this species is not as large as the mule deer. The great variation in its size is dependent on subspecies, region, availability and types of food, runting, and allied factors. As an example, an exceptional whitetail buck from the northeastern states may weigh 275 pounds or more. An average buck near the Mexican border in the Southwest usually weighs 80 to 90 pounds. An outstanding whitetail buck I once killed in the hill country of Texas had a 19½-inch antler spread and weighed 135 pounds.

The whitetail is a brush-loving deer and frequents more rolling and forested areas than his mountain cousin the mule deer. He depends for his survival more on eluding and outwitting enemies, including man, than does the mule deer, which tends to put more distance between himself and his enemies, once alerted. One indication of this is the fact that a great majority of whitetail deer are killed within 100 yards of the hunter, while distance shots across canyons and great open areas are common in mule-deer hunting. In his strategy to elude enemies, the whitetail ducks, skulks behind foliage, sneaks low to the ground, circles, doubles back, and lies low close to known danger — all in a canny effort to play hide-and-seek with man. His backtrack therefore becomes a maze rather than a trail such as that left by other species. This all adds to the difficulty of tracking and locating the animal.

The tracks of a large whitetail buck are similar to those of a big mule-deer buck, except that they are a trifle thinner. An exceptional whitetail

9

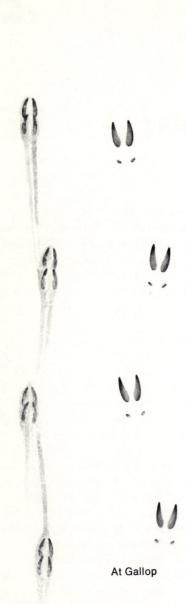

At Gallop

In Snow

Walking in snow, left, the whitetail leaves drag marks and double imprints. Individual imprints from a galloping deer show dewclaws and splayed hoofs, and the sets of four imprints occur at 6-foot intervals.

buck's front hoofs may leave an imprint of 2½ to 3 inches. To the experienced eye, the space between the halves of the front hoof is slightly wider than in the case of big mule-deer bucks. Like those of the mule and blacktail deer, the dewclaws of the whitetail's hoofs leave imprints only in mud, very soft earth, snow, or when the animal is running. In this last case, the halves of the hoofs splay out under the downward pressure of the animal's weight. The wide variation of size in whitetail tracks in the same area is determined by differences between fore and hind feet, the sex of the deer, and animal size. The tracks left by a whitetail doe or fawn in dry dust are often no more than tiny V's, the rear portion of the hoof leaving no imprint.

Once in a good whitetail country, where animals are known or expected to be, the hunter should use the tracks as an indication of the animal's presence and possible location rather than as an actual trail to the game. In fresh snow, following a track to the animal is a possibility, but will more often lead to disappointment. The wary whitetail can outsee, outhear, and outsmell man. Like the mule deer it plans its backtrack so as to detect all followers without being seen.

There are three basic techniques for finding whitetail deer in their brushy forest habitat. One is a driving method, whereby certain of the hunters are placed at key spots in the area, such as gully heads, rocks, and other elevations overlooking small canyons, or where a brushy area ends in open country. These are called standers, mainly because they do little more than remain completely mo-

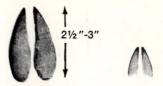

On dusty ground a mature buck's hoof makes a complete impression, left. But the lighter-weight doe or fawn leaves just a V-like track.

tionless and wait for the others to move deer into their vision and range. The other members of the group are called walkers or drivers. They proceed to the far end of a gully, brush patch, or other area to be driven, then move in a broad line toward the standers until eventually the two groups come together.

Since the whitetail's strategy is to circle and dodge, it is apt, after detecting the presence of the drivers, to move ahead for a way, then double back. This gives the drivers a chance to come close to the game. Otherwise, if the game moves on ahead, it will come to or pass the standers, giving them their chance.

Chiefly because of the dwindling game supply, driving is now rarely used to locate whitetail deer except by small parties of hunters.

A more sporting method perhaps is stalking. This must be done upwind and very slowly. The hunter learns of the presence of game by finding tracks and dung along the ridge trails, promontories, and gully sides. He then proceeds down very slowly, studying all foliage, movement, and coloration for sight of the game.

Frequently the sudden raucous chattering of a squirrel or cackling of a magpie will indicate that a deer is near. The hunter, however, must still detect the animal, either moving or standing, before it spots him. A basic consideration here is the fact that a man or animal spots movement less quickly when in motion than when stationary. The more motionless a hunter remains, the better able he is to spot a whitetail.

The experienced stalker knows that it is rare indeed to catch a com-

Pellet droppings about ¾-inch long are standard.

Rather than look for the whole animal, many successful hunters concentrate on picking out parts such as antlers, ears, or legs.

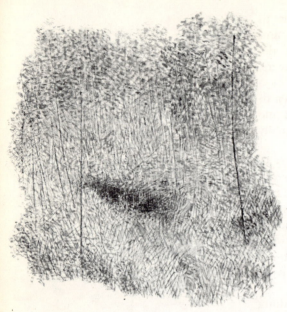

This is a typical bedding spot in brush and tall grass. A warm bed tells the hunter that he may be stalking a now alerted whitetail.

plete glimpse of a whitetail, unless it is rapidly crossing an opening. He is more likely to see a branch that looks too symmetrical, a shape, color, or upright line that does not quite belong. Upon painstaking scrutiny, the branch is seen to be an ear sticking out behind a tree, the shape slowly evolves into the outline of a deer's head, and the line becomes a deer's leg.

Many hunters reverse the hunting process and let a whitetail find them. This is done by stillhunting, or in other words by remaining perfectly quiet, while watching a ridge top, game trail, or other place where a whitetail is known or thought to be. Quietly stalking is also sometimes called stillhunting. One veteran whitetail hunter found that he was most successful when he combined these two techniques. He would stalk for an hour or so, then stop and stillhunt, watching his own backtrack. He had apparently taken numerous whitetails that had circled to watch him out of curiosity and were on his own backtrack.

Two-hunter strategy. In this heavily-wooded canyon, beginning at point A, hunter 1 could work the lower left side. Hunter 2 should then move just below the ridge crest on the right so that deer from below won't see him against the sky. Lagging a bit behind his partner, hunter 1 may spook a deer across canyon openings; or the deer may continue up the right side toward hunter 2. A deer spooked by hunter 2 may circle down toward hunter 1. Or an alerted animal may move slowly ahead of the hunters, finally exposing itself to one of them near the head of the canyon (B).

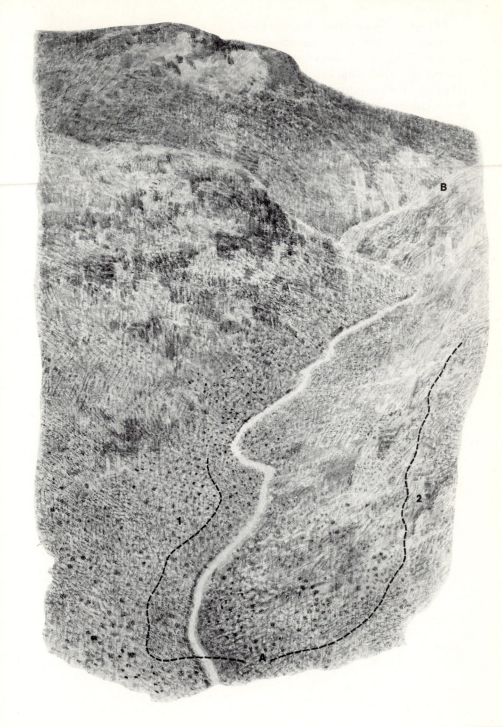

Different regions often develop their own technique for locating white-tail deer. For example, in the extensive mesquite, scrub-oak, and brushland areas of Texas, two novel methods of hunting whitetail bucks have been successfully used. One involves an old pair of shed deer antlers. A hunter takes the antlers into the hunting field, to a small opening between the brush patches where he is invisible to the deer. There, he rattles the antlers together, scratches the side of an oak with the tines as though scraping vel-vet and polishing the antlers for battle, or, grunting loudly, digs the tines into the rocky earth, simulating the battle of two bucks during the rut. Frequently, a rut-crazed old buck, unable to stand the sounds the competi-tion any longer, will literally jump into the opening and nearly onto the hunter.

A second method, in heavily brushed cactus country, is to build elevated stands. These, resembling small wooden huts, are reached by a high lad-der. Hunters, unable to walk into the surrounding cactus on foot, can then see from around 12 to 15 feet over the terrain and spot any deer moving about and coming their way.

In other wooded areas of the country, hunters often simply conceal themselves in brush-pile blinds artfully put together so as to resemble the surrounding foliage, and wait for a whitetail to come down the ridge, rim, crest, or runway.

3

Blacktail Deer

THE BLACKTAIL DEER *(Odocoileus hemionus columbianus)* is a third general species of deer found in North America. It is far less common than either the mule or whitetail deer and is found only in a large strip just inland from the Pacific Ocean, stretching from central California in the south to the northern tip of British Columbia, with its greatest depth at the Washington-Canada border.

The blacktail is more closely allied to the mule deer than to the whitetail. It is somewhat stocky in build like the mule deer, without the racy lines of the whitetail. In size, it is midway between the other two species. Adult deer weigh around 150 pounds, although an exceptional buck can weigh up to 250 pounds.

The tracks of a good blacktail buck measure up to 3 inches in length, excluding the dewclaws. Like those of other species of deer, the dewclaws of the blacktail show only when the tracks are made in soft earth, mud, or snow, or when the animal is running.

As with other species of deer, tracks are useful in helping to find the deer and should all be carefully "read." Large tracks in a single set are probably those of a buck. Smaller tracks of various sizes no doubt mean that a doe and fawns have passed that way. Large tracks intermingled with smaller ones may indicate that the fall rut is on, and the sexes are intermingling. Meandering tracks often mean the game is feeding, while straight tracks along a game trail or hillside imply that the game is headed for a place some distance off. Bounding tracks are an indication that the game is alerted, and if they persist as the hunter follows, he can presume that he was responsible for spooking the game.

The age of deer tracks is of importance to anyone looking for game, and many factors can influence their apparent age. Tracks in fresh snow, for example, are fluffy and soft in appearance, since the new-fallen snow moves with any disturbance, and flakes fall back into the tracks. Sharp-edged tracks, on the other hand, have generally been made in thawing or

15

weather-packed snow. If the snow in the bottom of the tracks is still unfrozen, the tracks must be relatively new. If such snow is icy or frozen, the tracks were probably made at least the night before. Deer tracks made in snow which has subsequently thawed appear enlarged, since the sides of the imprints thaw away in an outward direction.

Deer tracks made in the dry dust of a game trail can look deceptively fresh for days. However, rain quickly "ages" such tracks and can make them appear to be a week old when in fact they were made less than an hour before. It is easier to judge the age of tracks in mud or wet ground. In this case the air and sun tend to dry the crisp edges of the imprint, and the slight differences in dirt color give an indication of the track's age. If it takes a sprinkling of the same mud, tossed into the trail, an hour to dry to the same extent, then the track is an hour old.

Dung can also be read as to age. The droppings of blacktail deer are like those of the mule deer, though usually a trifle smaller. If the kernels resist pressure or crumble away upon being stepped on, the spoor is old. If, however, the kernels tend to matt together under one's boot, the dung is fresh, particularly if the color on its surface is precisely the same as that on the inside.

Since the blacktail deer favors the humid forest of the Pacific coastal area, many of the techniques for locating the game are comparable to those used in hunting whitetail deer in brush or thickly forested areas. Slow-stalking, after determining from the spoor that game is in the area, is a fine method for finding the animals. Stillhunting on much-used game trails, in gully heads, and on saddles between hills is also productive.

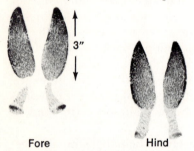

Fore   Hind

The tracks of the blacktail are similar to those of the mule deer, but are generally smaller. When the blacktail runs, its hoofs splay outward and the dewclaws register, as shown here.

Droppings of the blacktail are normally pellet-shaped and about ½ inch in diameter. When the deer is feeding on grasses, its scat becomes a homogeneous mass.

In either form of hunting, it is important to watch fringe areas especially in cut-over lands and old forest burns. Deer love to feed in the small meadows, creek beds, and low foliage that lie just outside timber and brush belts. The animals can find better food in these open fringe areas, where the sun produces more rapid growth than in shaded forests. Moreover, they have the safety factor of being able to bound quickly back into the protection of tree-cover.

A variation of the driving method for hunting whitetails works well with blacktails in heavy cover. This might be called the partner hunting method, with two or three individuals working together. Each hunter more or less "plays dog" for the others.

First a small basin, gully, canyon, or draw which shows fresh deer sign, or which simply appears promising, is chosen. Next, the direction of the wind is determined by holding a wet finger up to the wind. The side of the finger exposed to the wind becomes cooler. Once the wind direction has been established, the hunters proceed to "work" the gully, with their backs to the wind. Sometimes this necessitates circling around in a long walk to the canyon head. More often than not, however, any breeze will be up-canyon, and the direction of the hunt will therefore be uphill.

One person takes a ridge on one side of the gully and proceeds maybe a hundred yards along it. If only two are in the party, the second person, after allowing the first person a start, walks slowly up the bottom of the draw, or just beyond it and a short distance up the opposite side. If three people hunt together, the first starts out ahead up one rim of the draw; the second follows slightly behind in the bottom of the draw; and the third comes a comparable distance behind the second, but just under the op-

Fringe areas of cut- or burnt-over lands often provide browse and good hunting.

posite rim of the gully or basin. In such cases, the partners should not work in a straight line, at right angles to the canyon, but should always form a staggered or angling line across the draw.

Any blacktail in such a position may do one of several things. He may elect to stay hidden in the brush of the bottom. If so, the second hunter will come upon him. If the animal chooses, after detecting the first hunter, to break from the gully to the opposite side, the third man will probably see it. The lead person is also very likely to come upon the game in the bottom of the draw or while working the fringes of the ridge he is on.

Once they have worked out one gorge, gully, or draw, the hunters may alter positions and partner-hunt the next area in a similar fashion.

In heavily forested areas, another productive method for blacktail hunting is to work in circles. This technique necessitates working with a partner. Within an area of several hundred yards where deer are known or expected to be, the spot with the densest cover is chosen. Normally, this will be near the center. One hunter, preferably wearing camouflaged clothing, conceals himself in such a position that he can see in all directions. The second hunter simply makes a big circle around the general periphery of the area, hunting as he goes. Because of the deer's innate tendency to double back toward an area where he has been, the circling hunter, at some part of his movement, either locates game for himself or causes it to circle back toward the concealed hunter. Hunters often alternate positions, both to get relief from being in a cramped, immobile position as the center man and to even up any hunting advantage.

4

Black Bear

THE BLACK BEAR *(Euarctos americanus)* is one of our more interesting big-game species, partly because he is something of a clown, and also because his status has changed from that of a predator to the more noble classification of a big-game animal.

This bear is a medium-sized animal, the adults averaging around 250 pounds. The usual coloration runs from brown to jet black, and there may be cubs of different colors in the same litter. The cubs are born during hibernation and weigh little more than half a pound. Hibernation generally starts in November or December and lasts until mid-May, but these dates may vary according to region, lateness of season, and weather.

The black bear has a large distribution over widely scattered areas within the forty-eight contiguous states, practically all the wooded regions of Canada, and almost all of Alaska as far as the Arctic. States with the largest populations are Washington, California, Maine, and Colorado. The animal is found along a continuous strip that follows the Rocky Mountains from Canada to Mexico. There are scattered areas of bear population in the eastern States as far south as Florida.

The best place to find black bears is Canada, where their population is largest. A singular trait of the animal also has an influence on his whereabouts. The black bear is a great wanderer and is on the move virtually all the time that he is not in hibernation. Moreover his pelage is in prime condition only during the first three weeks after emergence from hibernation and from September to hibernation, thus limiting the time when he is pursued as a trophy or for photography purposes.

Black-bear tracks are unlike those of the hoofed species in that the fore and hind feet leave very different imprints. The front tracks consist of three elements, the pad, five toes, and claw marks. The pad is kidney-shaped, with the toe marks set in the front, and the claw marks fairly close to the imprint of the toes. In the hind track, however, the pad continues along the outside of the foot and ends in a definite heel. The track resem-

Black bears scratch and rub against old burns, and also rip them apart to eat ants, grubs, and wood worms.

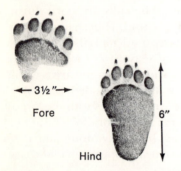

← 3½" →

Fore

6"

Hind

The forefoot track of the black bear is noticeably smaller than the hind; note the separations between the claws, toe pads and sole.

Bear scat may show berries, grass, roots, hair from carrion, or even wood debris after the bear has torn apart stumps to lap up insects.

bles that of a man with high-arched feet but is considerably smaller, measuring about 6 inches in the case of an adult bear.

Bear tracks are most easily seen and identified in soft earth, where they show up well. On rougher, harder terrain such as vegetation, leaves, and twigs they are difficult to identify. They are rarely found in snow, except by high-country hunters in late season, since with heavy snows the bear goes into winter hibernation. Occasionally one finds fresh bear tracks in a wet, early-season snowfall. Such tracks show up extremely well and are easy to identify.

Black bears like to saunter along stream beds, which provide such foods as carrion as well as an easy route to travel. This bear has a special liking for following trails, particularly those which horse- and man-travel have made dusty. This is because the pads of its feet are relatively tender. Often when searching along a mountainside for such food as wild huckleberries, a black bear will work down one ridge, strike a horse trail, wander along it for a hundred yards, then leave it to head up the next ridge. It is for this reason that many a black bear has been surprised by an equally startled person walking or riding on a mountain trail. The tracks a bear leaves after such an encounter are often most interesting. The bruin normally wheels around, as though on a swivel, and bounds off. As he does so, he seems to reach far up and out under his extended chin with his forefeet, grabbing a hunk of earth with his claws, then throwing it backward behind his hind feet in a great bound. At the same time his hind feet come forward alongside his chin, grab more earth, and likewise throw it back. The gait is aptly known as "scissoring."

During years of wild-berry abundance, black bears normally range high in mountain country. They meticulously strip off the ripened fruit and work the heavy-bearing patches until the fruit drops. When wild fruit is scarce, they work farther down and are often found along stream beds looking for food. During such years, one may be sure that any campsites in the area, especially abandoned ones, will be visited by "pest" black bears. Often by hunting both sides of a canyon bounding a recently-raided camp, especially at dawn and dusk, one can locate the guilty bear.

Old abandoned ranches in outlying country where there were once fruit orchards are a favorite haunt of black bears. Miners in the early days planted orchards around their shacks in order to make applejack. There are remains of some of these old orchards and shacks in the Middle Salmon River country, and here numerous broken branches often prove that a black bear has climbed the trees to get at the ripening apples.

The black bear also likes old burns in forest country, where the stumps have rotted with age. A bear will go methodically from one stump to another, ripping them apart and eating the ants, white grubs, and wood-worms that have colonized them. Often the stumps look as though they had been torn open with the toe of an ax. A good way to find a bear in an old blackened burn is to study the spot carefully with binoculars from across the valley or gully. Frequently the stump that one has been looking at along with dozens of others suddenly moves off and becomes a grub-digging bear.

Black bears, in game country, always sooner or later come to investigate the offal left from kills of such game as deer, moose, and elk. They find this offal in one of two ways. Either the offal ripens after a few days and sends odors into the breezes that a black bear can smell from a great distance; or the bear finds the animal remains through a form of wilderness telegraphy. Predatory magpies find the offal of any kill within a few hours at most. They cackle the news to the wandering coyotes, who find the feast and yodel the fact into the air. Thus the bear hears it and proceeds to the offal or carrion. It is therefore often productive to watch such animal remains.

Because black bears are always wandering around, usually alone and grumpy, since the sexes mingle only during the mating season, it is hard to predict just where one may be; and because of their relative rarity in the lower forty-eight states, one of the best ways to locate them is incidentally. That is, while camping, fishing, backpacking, or hunting other species of game, one simply "runs into" a bear. By deliberately choosing for the other outdoor activities, country where bears are known to be, one very often locates his bruin in an effortless way. As an example, my own first black was killed while we were hunting elk. The huge blackie was eating an elk quarter when we returned from hunting, and I took him. Another black bear was taken after he had spooked a great six-point mule-deer buck I was stalking. I shot the bear instead of the buck.

There is one exciting feature of tracking a black bear. That is, one can always tell with near certainty just how big the bear is through the knowledge of one simple formula. By measuring across the front pad of a bear's track, then adding the figure one and changing the inches to feet, one can tell in advance just how big his bear rug will be. For instance, if the front pad of the bear being tracked measures 5 inches across, then the anticipated bear rug will measure 6 feet square.

5

Grizzly Bear

THE GRIZZLY BEAR *(Ursus horribilis)* is one of our most respected and romanticized big-game animals. This is due to his large size, ferocity, and unpredictable nature. The grizzly bear fears nothing, and a fight with him is normally to the death.

The average grizzly may weigh around 400 pounds, though unusual specimens have weighed up to a half-ton. This bear is characterized by his varied color, which may range from a creamy tan to badgery silver, dark brown, and black. His spine has silvery guard hairs that give him his nickname of "silvertip." The grizzly also has a dish-face, long claws that extend far out over his fore toe pads, and a noticeable hump at his withers.

Civilization has driven the solitude-loving grizzly bear into our remaining remote areas. While a grizzly is not afraid of man, he is wary by nature and prefers to be left entirely alone. The species is on the decrease and is now found only in the most rugged mountain country on the continent. A few grizzlies remain in the rough mountains of the Northwest, mainly in Montana, and the rest are to be found in western Canada, Alaska, the Yukon, and the Northwest Territories. When locating this species, one's efforts should be planned in these areas. Local information from inhabitants, professional guides, and experienced hunters can help to narrow down the regions where one may expect to find one of the great bears.

Within the limited areas of grizzly populations, there are signs that help to indicate the presence of the game. Female grizzlies mate only in alternate years and do not mingle with the opposite sex except during the mating season. For this reason, adults often travel alone, except for the sow with cubs, so any grizzly sign found is likely to be that of a solitary animal.

Like black bears, grizzlies are great wanderers and travel miles in search of food. A silvertip will establish an area of up to 15 miles across that he periodically works. Along the boundaries of the area, the bear marks certain trees with his claws, as high as he can reach, to show that he considers this his private domain. Moreover he often uses these trees as rubbing posts, to

Grizzly bears conceal their kill with sticks, branches, and mud, and return to the cache until the whole carcass is consumed.

Fore

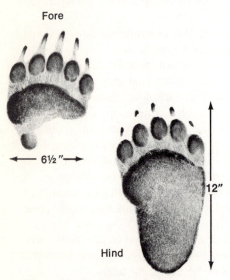

←— 6½ ″ —→

Hind

12″

Tracks of the grizzly bear are much larger, and the claws thicker, than those of the black bear.

Grizzly scat is unsegmented and up to 2 inches in diameter. Piles are half-gallon size.

work out the loose, shaggy hair from his hide after winter hibernation. Often these rubbing trees are spruces, whose sticky excretions help pull out the hair. Any other grizzly infringing on such a territory is courting a savage fight, and any trespassing black bear is chased and killed by the grizzly, if he can catch the intruder. Thus the presence of black bears in an area normally means that there is no grizzly there. Conversely, absence of black bears in likely black-bear country may indicate the presence of a grizzly.

The grizzly's private territory is often bounded by the high ridges surrounding some great Canadian or Alaskan basin. His tracks may be found along the game trails of these ridges or in other areas of soft dirt. Often the tracks in muskeg, tundra, or other lush ground-cover in bush country show only as depressions in the vegetation and cannot be surely identified. Grizzly tracks will also show up in the silt along the shores of glacial creeks, which this bear frequents in search of wild peavines.

The grizzly's tracks are comparable to those of the black bear, except that they are more thickset. Front tracks run from 6 to 6½ inches in width, and hind tracks reach 12 inches. The huge grizzlies in the 8- to 9-foot class are largely creatures of the past. Today a 7-foot bear is a good specimen. The formula already given for estimating the size of black bears applies also to grizzlies. Thus an 8-foot bear will have a front footpad measuring 7 inches across.

The best aid for finding grizzlies, once one is in known grizzly country, is a good pair of high-powered binoculars. Eight-power is a good size. It is virtually impossible to locate a grizzly bear from his tracks. Except in the rare cases where early snow has fallen, tracking over the rough grizzly terrain is beyond human ability and stamina. Instead, one should determine from the spoor the size of the bear, the general direction in which he is headed, where he is most likely to go, and if he is working any specific area. Then, on the basis of the animal's habits and likely field behavior, the hunter should look the country over until the bear is spotted.

In spring hunting, the slide areas left by avalanches are spots where grizzlies are most apt to appear first. The vegetation in these areas comes up first, often on the tail of melting snows. There the great beasts scout for the first green grasses and the plants such as dogtooth violets that are necessary to their digestive systems after winter hibernation. The best way to hunt slide areas is to locate them with the glasses, then move to a vantage point on the opposite side of the basin or valley and from there study them for both bear and bear signs such as fresh diggings. Bears will also frequent any stream beds in the area at this time of year, both for possible food and as a means of crossing basins and valleys. The best times to watch are during the early morning and at dusk.

The meadowlands in high mountain country, which produce grasses at about the same time, are another good place to watch. Grizzlies dig in them, in both spring and fall, in their search for grubs and rodents. Often an entire half-acre patch will be dug up methodically, as though with a shovel.

Among the best places to locate a grizzly in the fall are the open hilltops and saddles just above the timberline that are common in the North. There snow often remains in patches, the source of glacial creeks farther down, and the bears dig for rodents such as the whistling marmot. These areas, open to view except for the short arctic birch, and the numerous canyon heads just off them are prime grizzly country. One should study such areas for hours with glasses from the valley below or a vantage point across the basin, since the undulations of the hilltops may often hide a bear busily digging for rodents.

Spotting a grizzly's movement is aided by the bear's glossy hide, which remains in good shape for three weeks after emergence from hibernation. Often the arctic birch, which grows to around 30 inches high, will hide an entire moving bear except where his back shows in a gap in the foliage. In bright sunlight, the shining, silvery spinal hairs are often visible before any other part of the animal.

One should also listen intently in grizzly country, especially in the fall when the bears are gorging on marmots, their last food before hibernation. The sudden, excited whistling or chirping of these large rodents sometimes indicates that a grizzly is chasing them or digging around the den area.

Another good place to look for fall grizzlies is a berry patch. In Alaska and Canada, in August and September, the ripe berries occur in patches often covering several acres of mountainside. These may be studied minutely from a shady vantage point across a basin or valley. When a grizzly finds a large patch of especially thick berries, such as the huge blueberries and wild raspberries of the North, he stays within the immediate vicinity for hours at a time, stripping the fruit off with his mouth. Careful glassing of these areas, even from great distances, will show any bear working them. Once spotted, the animal can be carefully stalked.

When any animal dies or is shot in grizzly country, one may be sure that a bear will find the remains shortly after. The grizzly's method is to drag the entire carcass into the closest concealment, then mound it over the sticks, branches, and often mud. He then eats at the carcass until it is gone. Such spoils may include animals up to the size of the great northern moose. Often, the huge bear remains near the carcass, lying concealed in heavy brush. He may also lie down on top of the carcass that he has mounded up, protecting it against any intruding bear. Within a day or so, the carcass bloats up and smells to high heaven. It is a cardinal rule in grizzly country to remember that a stink in bush country means a dead carcass and a grizzly on top of it, ready to fight. There is no overrating a grizzly's ferocity in such an encounter. A hunter should always mark down his game kills in bear country, and approach them subsequently with the greatest cautions, since a grizzly may have found the kill.

The grizzly's dung is a vital factor in the tracking and locating of the bear. The dung is unsegmentized, up to 2 inches in diameter, and is found in piles averaging about a half-gallon. Dung that is purple in color and full of seeds indicates that the bear is feeding largely on wild fruit. Numerous piles of dung in a small area mean that the bear is returning to work that area frequently. If there is little difference in color between the outside and inside of the pile when it is scattered, then the bear that deposited it is not far away.

6

Brown Bear

SOME AUTHORITIES, claiming that there is little scientific difference between the grizzly and the brown bear, have grouped them in the same classification. Outdoorsmen, however, have always considered the brown or "Kodiak" bear *(Ursus middendorffi)* to be separate species of big game. This is because the bear's habitat is different, as are his habits, and he is a far larger bear. His tracks and other spoor are similar to but larger than the grizzly's.

Brown bears of 10 and 11 feet are now extremely rare, owing to limited range and hunting pressure, but there are still 8- and 9-foot brownies left. A brown bear with an 8-inch front pad will furnish a hide 9 feet square. Such a bear, immediately after hibernation, weighs around 1,000 pounds, and after a summer's feeding on salmon it reaches 1,200 pounds.

The brown bear's range extends over the southeastern coastal region of Alaska, running about 75 miles inland and including many of the larger offshore islands such as Kodiak, Admiralty, Chichagof, Afognak, Unimak, and Baranof. The island of Kodiak is especially well-known for its brown bear and gives the animal his nickname of Kodiak bear.

When attempting to locate this magnificent game animal, one should first narrow the overall range down as much as possible. A good way to do this is to study hunting maps and the game regulations issued by the Alaska Fish and Game Commission. These will show the areas where brown bear may be pursued, and a concentrated effort may then be made in one such area. The next step is to contact a reliable outfitter who knows and hunts that particular region. An outfitter is necessary when hunting brown bear, both to satisfy legal requirements for the nonresident and to provide the equipment needed for a successful hunt for either the local or nonresident hunter.

Once in brown-bear country, two methods are used in locating the animals. One technique is to scout the islands and mainland from just offshore with a suitable boat, studying all terrain with high-power glasses. Once a bear is located, as he moves about along some high slope, the boat

Brown bear trails are visible through muskeg and are commonly found in the fall season near salmon spawning streams.

puts in to shore a considerable distance away, so as not to disturb the animal. A temporary camp is made near the shore there, and then the hunters stalk the animal. Often in the past, large outfitters used boats that served as floating camps once they had been moved into some bay, out of sight of any bear spotted.

The second method is to make a more or less permanent camp in known bear country, then stalk the animals by first glassing all surrounding high basins from a suitable vantage point on the opposite side. This is done with high-powered binoculars or the smaller portable spotting scopes. The bears move around feeding until 9 or 10 A.M., then go into deep cover to shade up during the heat of the day. Then about 2 to 3 P.M. they again emerge from cover, to continue feeding. Anyone seriously stalking a brownie should be prepared to wait all day if necessary. It is best to wear camouflage clothing and take along some item such as a space blanket for protection from the chilly ocean breezes.

Spring and fall are the two appropriate seasons to hunt brown bear. The spring is preferable for several reasons. First, at this time of the year, while their hides are still in prime condition after emergence from hibernation in May, the great bears can

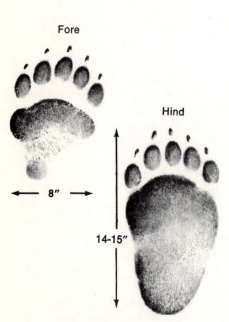

Fore

Hind

8"

14-15"

The tracks of the brown bear are similar to those of the grizzly, but they are much larger.

easily be spotted. Grass is a necessary element of their diet after long hibernation, and they therefore frequent the great, high tracts of country where alder patches alternate with open areas of grass. As they move over the grass or even through the dense alder thickets, they can usually be spotted with glasses from an opposing slope. Furthermore, at this

The normal scat of the brown bear consists mostly of grasses.

season they are usually still around their winter dens, and the dumpings from these, where they have hollowed out earth from some sunny alpine slope, may be spotted. Their great tracks, over the remaining snow patches are easily seen with a spotting scope. A bear may well lie out to sun himself in the semiopen of a big snow patch, where he is easily seen at high elevations. Or he may simply toboggan downward over a snow patch to reach an area below, leaving a long, broad depression in the snow that is visible for miles. These optimum conditions exist during the late May-early June period while the alders are still bare of leaves. Hence both game and its signs are more easily seen. A final important reason for spring hunting is that the bears at this season are on the move looking for sows, and bears are far easier to spot on the move than immobile.

Once a bear is located, a stalking strategy must be planned, preferably for the early morning or evening. To approach a brownie shaded up in heavy alders is most difficult. He normally chooses the thickest, most snow-flattened patches for the purpose, and as the hunter tries to negotiate a passage through the alders and the maze of wild raspberry bushes usually mixed in with them, the noise will give his presence away.

In early June, the leaves on the alders begin to come out, and within a couple of weeks they effectively prevent the distant spotting and identification of any bears wandering around in the alders. By then, however, the pelage of the bears has begun to be rubbed, and there is no real purpose in stalking the game.

With summer, the salmon runs begin. Then the great bears usually move and feed on the fish that come up into the small inland creeks and streams to spawn. It is easy in summer for a brownie to wade in these creeks and grab a flopping meal. It is this fish diet which, some think, makes the brown bear more amiable than his short-tempered relative the grizzly.

Because of the salmon runs, the early fall is another good season for locating brown bear. At this time many of the animals are still hanging around the salmon streams, and stalking up the gravelly creek beds is very often productive. During fall, too, the bears will be found around the coastline, scouting for food, as well as moving upward, later, toward eventual hibernation. The fringes of the vast grassy expanses between alder patches are another good area to look for them at this season.

In any brown-bear hunting, the wind is a vital factor. As with other species, any stalking or moving about should be done into the wind. A brown bear can pick up the scent of a human from a great distance.

Because of the enormous desirability of the brown bear as a trophy, which has resulted in growing hunting pressure, and because of the recent increase of military and commercial aviation around the best bear areas, this animal has developed an intense wariness. Some of the really big bears remain, and their tracks are sometimes found in snow patches, along creek beds, and in the widespread "buggy-tracks" made by other bears. It is increasingly difficult, however, to see the animals themselves because they have learned to feed at night, when darkness protects them from human molestation. They come out of the alder patches only when dusk approaches and are back in hiding shortly after daybreak.

7

Shiras Moose

THE SHIRAS MOOSE *(Alces americana shirasi)* is found mainly in the West, in a narrow strip of country running down from Canada through the states of Wyoming, Montana, and Idaho. Within this general area, the species likes low hills and plateaus well-forested with conifers and aspens and containing many streams, lakes, and swampy areas. Two typical examples of moose habitat are the well-watered, pine-forested Island Park country in Idaho, adjacent to Yellowstone Park, and the willow-covered meadowlands along the upper reaches of the Green River in Wyoming.

Nature could hardly have designed a more homely big-game animal than the Shiras moose. Nevertheless, his ungainly features serve a purpose in his survival, as well as help to locate and identify him. The lanky legs enable him to cross fallen timber and wade through deep water and snow. His large ears permit him to hear enemies from afar, and his great overhanging lip is well-adapted to stripping off the leaves and twigs from high willows and aspen trees, on which he partly lives.

What the moose lacks in beauty he makes up for in size. The bigness of the animal makes both tracking and locating him easier and increases his appeal to the big-game hunter. Bull moose of this species weigh around 1,200 pounds and occasionally have an antler spread of as much as 52 to 54 inches. The animal is dark brown in color, with some nearly black areas and lighter brown-roan legs that can easily be mistaken for small tree boles. When a Shiras moose is being tracked in heavy timber, the legs are an important identification feature.

While elk tracks and the front tracks of mule-deer bucks are round and chunky in appearance, the halves of a moose's hoofs are slim in outline and more widely spaced. A large bull Shiras moose leaves a front track measuring up to 5½ or 6 inches in length. In the soft earth and mud where his spoor is often seen, the dewclaws leave an imprint. When the animal breaks into his long, swinging trot, the hoof halves splay out. Like several other species of big game whose foreparts, including the antlers, are heavier than their hind parts, the moose has front hoofs that are larger than the hind ones. Again as with other species, the females leave slightly smaller tracks than the males. In poor tracking conditions, the dung of the moose helps greatly to distinguish the species from domestic cattle and wild elk. Moose dung is segmented, the oval kernels measuring ¾ inch or more in diameter. When the moose is on a diet of aspen and willow, the dark olive dung is lighter in color than that of elk.

The moose's food consists chiefly of the leaves and younger stems of aspens and willows and of aquatic vegetation that the animals pull up from the bottom of streams and lakes.

·One can learn a vast amount on how to track and locate this animal by knowing its daily routine. This is more or less stabilized within good moose country, since the animals hardly have a winter and summer migration, as elk do in some areas.

At daylight, the animals often feed on bottom vegetation, standing up to their withers in a river with a slow current or in a shallow lake. At mid-morning, they leave the streams or lakes in order to shade up during the heat of the day. Often they stand while shading up, but occasionally one will catch them lying down. For this part of the day, they like knolls or timbered promontories overlooking the stream beds, lakes, or meadowland where they have fed. They do not move more than a mile or so from the good feeding areas, to which they return at twilight to feed once more.

This basic cycle can be read from their great tracks, which are to be found in any game trails along streams or lakeshores, and often at the spots where the animals have gone into the water. They can also be traced into the nearby timbered knolls and foothills where the animals spend the day.

During the mating season, the adult bulls become very pugnacious. Often, as a fisherman or other outdoorsman comes around the brushy bend of a river, he may meet such a bull face to face. The bull's long mane bristles usually come up, and he is very apt to charge and chase the surprised intruder up the handiest tree.

During the rut, a bull's presence can often be established in the brushy or willow-covered country along a lakeshore simply by cupping the hands around the mouth and making a guttural, coughing call, sounding like *U-u-waugh! U-u-waugh!* This is a battle challenge, and any rut-crazed bull within hearing is likely to crash forth out of the brush and come at a swinging trot toward the sound. Another trick that will sometimes attract a bull in the neighborhood is to pour a hatful of water into the calm water of a lake at dusk. This simulates the urination of the cow and generates immediate interest in a bull.

Shiras moose can be located incidentally while one is hunting elk or other big-game mountain species on horseback. Hunting camps are normally established at the lower elevations, and the actual hunting for elk and mule deer is usually done higher up. After scouting the lower creek-bed and stream areas for moose, the hunter climbs for the greater part of the day after his principal species. As he comes back down after the day's hunt, he may well locate moose that have come out into the meadows and lower stream country to feed.

Shiras moose are fairly easy to track in snow because of their great hoofprints and the fact that they normally do not travel very far. As with deer and some other species, it is best to track parallel to the spoor at a distance of 50 yards or so from it. Moose, too, watch their backtrack. It is possible, however, and sometimes necessary, to trail a moose step by step directly on its track until the animal is come upon. This is particularly the case in snow. Often the tracker's glance will take in a number of tracks at once, making it unnecessary to examine each imprint closely. Even in snow, however, the tracker may come upon individual tracks that do not look like those of a moose. Light snow may have fallen back into the imprint and blurred its contour, possibly when the animal went through brush or willows. Or, as it stepped, the moose may have kicked up dirt and mixed it with the snow.

The tracking technique is to anticipate, from the animal's general stride and direction, approximately where the next imprint should be and there search for it, regardless of how it looks. It should be remembered, however, that the animal may suddenly pause, stop, turn, browse a bit, or move off in an entirely new direction.

Whenever the tracker comes upon any place where the next imprint of a trail does not show for some reason, he should stop at the last plain track and make a mental circle all around it, having a radius the same length as the animal's stride. A close examination of this circle will usually disclose the next track, which may often show up not as a clear imprint, but as a depression in the leaves, an overturned leaf or small rock, a broken twig, or just the curved outline of one side of a hoof. If, somewhere around this mental circle, a track does not appear in some form, then the circle should be enlarged to a radius of two normal steps and a similar search made around the circumference of the larger circle.

If no succeeding tracks can be picked up in this way, or in areas of rock or water where imprints cannot be left, it becomes necessary to cast about in a much larger circle. If the tracker makes an arc across the presumed path of the trail about a rod or even a hundred yards or more from where he has temporarily lost the tracks, he can usually pick up the trail again.

A moose trail will often lead into a thick patch of willows, a bog, or even water, perhaps in some low, brushy creek bottom where the tracker cannot or does not wish to go. To find out if the animal has crossed the area or is still in it, his best method is to circle the spot until he reaches the place where the animal would probably have emerged. He should then cast about in suitably sized circles until he picks up the tracks again. If the animal is still in the impenetrable area, the lack of tracks emerging on the far side will indicate the fact.

A moose will often wade into a small creek or even a small lake, then wander along in the water after having changed direction entirely, and finally emerge either on the opposite bank or even on the side where it en-

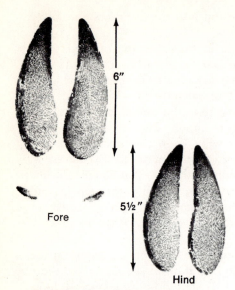

6"

5½"

Fore

Hind

The Shiras moose's hoofs are slim in outline and more widely spaced than those of an elk or mule deer.

tered. In such cases, the tracker must move along the shoreline on both sides of the water and in both directions, until he finds the spot where the tracks emerge. If the animal has left the water recently, drops of water off its body will still be visible along the tracks.

In the step-by-step trailing of a moose, or any other wild game, the tracker should move slowly so as not to alarm the animal somewhere up ahead. More important, perhaps, he should alternate his study of the tracks with scrutiny of the area ahead of him, to catch sight, if possible, of the animal as it watches its backtrack.

There is a bonus advantage to tracking a species by trailing it. As a hunter pursues a certain animal, he is likely to locate not only the animal he is tracking but also others of the same or even different species.

The technique of tracking moose by trailing them is comparable to the tracking of many other game species.

8

Alaska Moose

THE ALASKA MOOSE *(Alces gigas)* is the largest of the three species of North American moose. Adult moose of the Kenai subspecies, found on the Kenai Peninsula, can weigh over a ton. The recorded antler spreads of some exceptional bulls have measured over 6 feet, though the average spread is around 60 to 65 inches.

The tracks of a large bull are prodigious, reaching 7 inches in length, excluding the imprint of the dewclaws. Because of the animal's great weight, the toes of the hoofs are splayed to some extent even during walking. When trotting, the hoofs splay to around 30 degrees.

In looking for these great animals, both the tracks and sightings are used, and good binoculars are a vital aid. Alaska moose wander over great areas of country, especially during the rut, but in much of their range, identifiable moose tracks are often hard to find. Much of the country is muskeg, interspersed with such vegetation as scrub popple, a high type of willow, and scrub spruce that often grows no higher than 15 to 20 feet. The muskeg is often over permafrost, and tracks in it tend to be quickly filled with water or obscured by the vegetation springing back. Moreover, the extreme sponginess of muskeg terrain will soon exhaust any foot-hunter who tries to travel over it more than a short distance.

The best places to look for moose tracks in this country are the rocks and sand of glacial creek beds, the shorelines of any lakes, ponds, or swampy areas, and especially the old game trails that often run just inside the timber or bush fringing the banks of creeks and rivers. Moose like to move just inside the protection of such foliage as they follow watercourses, studying the bottom areas or debating whether to cross a basin bottom. They particularly favor those large areas of Alaska willow that surround or touch upon lakes, creeks, or rivers. The huge willows, often twice the height of a man, provide not only a large part of their food, but also the concealment that the animals instinctively crave. Their range varies in general elevation from low, swampy areas to the lower benchlands and rolling, timbered hills, but rarely extends to more mountainous terrain.

Hunting this giant species is basically comparable to hunting the Canadian and Shiras moose. The early morning and late evening are best, as the animals tend to move out of the shade then. Lake, river, and creek-bed areas are the most productive, and the foot-hunter should follow shoreline trails and the open courses of glacial streams.

While searching these areas for sign, the tracker should also hunt the animals visually. The huge size of this moose makes him easy to spot whenever his color contrasts with that of the terrain or foliage. When standing against a backdrop of open glacial wash, along a creek bed, or when wading

In dense timber the tracker often first notices the bull's antlers, reflecting sunlight.

offshore in a lake a moose stands out like a barn. But when seen against, or partially hidden by dark Alaska spruces, the animal is far harder to detect. A moose moving, in any kind of terrain, is far easier to spot than one standing immobile.

Horses are being used increasingly in Alaska for hunting purposes and have become almost a necessity for hunting moose. A big, strong horse that has been born or raised in muskeg country can plod over the boggy terrain all day, whereas a mile of such travel in the marshier areas would exhaust the foot-hunter. Horses are handy also for fording the numerous streams, wading along the shallow shorelines of lakes where there are no trails, and negotiating blowdown timber.

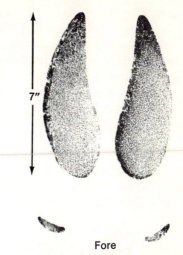

Fore

The Alaska moose has the largest tracks of all hoofed animals. Due to the animal's weight, its hoofs splay, as above, even at a walk. Running tracks splay about 30 degrees.

There is another special reason for looking for moose on horseback. Horses that are trained to hunt develop a keen sense of game. Often a horse will smell, hear, or sight game far more quickly than a man. When this happens, a good horse used in game country will prick up his ears, turn his head in the direction where he spots something, and generally stop in his stride. Moreover, in low bush country Indian guides often stop the horse, stand upright on the saddle and sight game from this vantage point, which allows them to see many more acres of bush. Similarly, by periodically climbing one of the taller spruces in the bush and willow country that moose frequent, the hunter may spot the dark back or swinging antlers of a bull moose that he would otherwise pass by.

Another trick is to learn to tell by the relative freshness of moose pawings how close the game may be. During the rut, a bull moose will occasionally find a spot of soft earth and paw a shallow depression in it maybe 3 feet across. In this depression he then urinates, before rolling or wallowing in it. By the freshness of the pawings, including that of the root-ends sticking out of the earth, the closeness of the bull can sometimes be determined. On one occasion, three of us came upon a bull actually rolling in the pawed-out spot, and my companion took movies. On another occasion, my Indian guide saw such a depression, dismounted, and put his nose down to within a foot to smell. When he rose, he said, "Big bull. Here two hours ago. Maybe a mile up the valley." A half-hour later, after riding up the valley bottom, we spooked the big beast as he watched his backtrack.

A good time to look for Alaska moose is about a week to ten days following the first hard frost of the season. In much of Alaska this normally occurs during the week around the 6th of September. Soon after this first heavy frost, the leaves of the big Alaska willow begin to fall, and before long the trees are bare. The gray of the naked stalks contrasts sharply with the bark-brown color of the moose. By using high-powered glasses, a tracker can now scrutinize the vast areas of leafless willow from some vantage point and locate any moose either standing or moving among the foliage from over a mile away. Ten days before, a rider could have passed unwittingly with his horse within 50 feet of a moose standing in a willow bed.

Tracking is further facilitated by the fact that the rut begins about this time. At this season, the great bulls start to travel great distances, night and day, in search of the cows. Often the nocturnal grunting and crashing of the mature bulls in the bush can aid in the location of the animals.

Canadian Moose

THE CANADIAN MOOSE *(Alces americana americana)* is the second largest species of moose in North America. It was once found in large numbers in the east of the United States, but, with the onset of civilization there and the massive cutting of the forests, it made a mass movement northward. It is one species that will probably remain abundant for a long time. It now inhabits a vast area, reaching from the Atlantic in the east to Alaska in the northwest, and embracing well over half the forested central area of Canada. All moose require great areas of cold, wooded country, and Canada with its forests, lakes, and cool climate provides an ideal habitat for this species. Moreover, the country is sparsely populated, and the huge animals can thrive there without too much molestation from man.

The species also lends itself well to transplanting in favorable regions. For example, the largest moose herd in the East is a transplanted one in Newfoundland. In 1878 and 1904, sportsmen released 9 moose in that mooseless area. Since 1935, over 100,000 moose have been taken from the island, and the population is still thriving.

In size, the Canadian moose is intermediate between the Shiras and the Alaska moose. The big bulls of this species measure nearly 7 feet at the withers, and exceptional specimens have an antler spread of 6 feet. The tracks are similar to those of the Shiras moose, but slightly larger. An adult bull's forefoot measures up to 6½ inches, not counting the dewclaws. These often leave an imprint in the soft earth around lakes and in the muskeg over which the animals travel.

This moose has an overall brown-black coloration, with lighter color around the muzzle and on the lower legs. His dark color is ideally suited to the wooded regions in which he spends a large part of the day. Unless a moose is moving, his great form merges with the deep shadows.

Like other species of deer, the moose is nocturnal in nature, though he spends the early daylight and dusk hours feeding. Like other moose species, the Canadian variety is never found too far from waters of some

The Canada moose is never far from water and favors wooded areas where lakes provide both food and protection from enemies. Track size is midway between that of the Alaska and the Shiras.

kind. These provide the moose with food in the form of aquatic vegetation and also afford him protection from enemies and from heat and flies during the summer months. Often a moose will escape out into the depths of a lake from a running pack of timber wolves, or will stand out there to escape the insects, so deeply immersed in water that only his withers and the top of his face show.

The first way to locate moose is by a form of trail-hunting, concentrating on the watery areas that the moose like. Any lake that is used by moose will have moose trails around the shorelines. Such trails are usually in the soft earth near water, and identification of the spoor is normally easy. The great weight of moose upon soft earth makes for deep, well-defined imprints. Normally, any moose traveling a lake-edge trail will not be running, and a slow walking gait adds to the definition of any game's track. Moreover, there will be occasional droppings, and these, too, are easy to read. The larger Canadian moose leaves dung almost identical to that of the Shiras moose, though somewhat larger.

By moving slowly upwind along the lake trails and those following meadowland creeks, and by carefully watching everything up ahead, a tracker can usually spot any moose in the water or near the trails as he goes along. It is wise, too, to listen as one travels. The slight dripping sounds of a moose wading or feeding in water indicate the presence of one or more of the animals not too far way.

Game trails can be used to advantage, too, in such areas as necks of land between two lakes, low saddles on adjacent ridges, and especially low, timbered benchlands, knolls, and promontories overlooking lakes and streams. Moose particularly like such areas when they are adjacent to the inlets and outlets of sizable lakes where the waters are usually shallower than in other places. Moose trails are generally found leading from these shallows to the deeper timber where the animals shade up.

Even in deeper timber areas, through which this species often travels, the movement of the animals will show during the rut or as they retreat from enemies. The trail areas are good places to find or slow-stalk a moose. Moose, like other species of wild game, are marvelous trail makers in that they habitually find and use the easiest routes through timber and over rough elevations. Not only is the moose tracker more likely to locate the animals near the routes they have made and use, but also he can travel easily on such trails.

In searching for moose in deep timber, a good trick is to look constantly for the deepest, blackest shadows. A moose standing in dense timber looks like a shadow, except that he is darker. The antlers of a big bull are often what one sees first in timber. The cross palms of the antlers do not quite look like tree branches or the numerous uplifted tines like willow saplings.

In areas where there are many large lakes, canoe-hunting for moose has long been popular. Hunters first ascertain the presence of moose in an area from the shoreline tracks, then use the canoe to paddle noiselessly around just offshore on the windy side of the lake, while watching for moose up ahead. All promontories are carefully rounded, close in to shore, as moose may well be in the shallow water of the next cove. The best periods of the day for this type of hunting are early mornings, when fog and mist on the water are likely to aid a close approach, and at dusk, when moose like to feed in the shallows.

Canada has in the past been ravaged by great burns which have wiped off thousands of acres of timber, leaving vast blackened scars. These regularly grow back with fireweed, scrub popple, and other lush vegetation which moose love once it has reached a reasonable growth. Where appropriate, they will often use an old burn as a thoroughfare between lakes. A good place from which to look for Canadian moose in one of these burns is a knoll, a ridge, or the side of a wide basin or valley that presents an open view. Good binoculars, preferably 6- to 8-power, are a great asset here.

There are two main things to look for when trying to locate a moose in a burn. The first is the general outline of the animal. If the second growth is not too high, one should carefully glass any lateral black form or line, as opposed to the generally vertical dark shapes of the burn. Depending upon the foliage height, one may see the animal's entire body or just the line of the back, head, and antlers. A second thing to watch for, in the fall, is the sight of antlers. At this time of the year, the velvet of the mature bulls has all been rubbed off, and the antler surface is tan and smooth. It reflects light quite like a mirror, at distances of over a mile. This dull white gleam, which intermittently appears and disappears, is pronounced against any backdrop of green timber. It comes from the changing angle of the animal's head, as he feeds on high foliage. Once spotted, he may then be stalked.

10

Elk

THE AMERICAN ELK *(Cervus canadensis)*, like the grizzly bear, has been driven by advancing civilization into the most remote areas. The present distribution of the elk extends through the Rocky Mountains, from Arizona in the south to Alberta, Canada, in the north. It also includes other smaller, scattered populations in California, Oregon, Washington, British Columbia, Saskatchewan, and Manitoba. This noble game animal has lent itself well to transplanting, under optimum conditions, to certain areas in the east and southwest of the United States and to such islands off Alaska as Afognak.

The elk, or wapiti, is majestic in appearance, with a tan body, brown neck hairs, a yellowish rump, an uplifted head, and regal antlers. Some adult bulls weigh nearly 1,000 pounds, measure almost 5 feet at the withers, and have an antler spread of nearly 50 inches.

In order to track and locate this species, one must, of course, be able to identify the animals at sight and confine the search to the limited regions of elk habitation.

The track of a bull elk is broader than that of moose, deer, and some other hoofed game. It measures from 3½ to 4 inches in length, not counting the dewclaws, which show in the imprint only when the animal is walking in soft terrain or running. At first sight, the contour of a bull-elk's track resembles a coffee cup split down the middle. Since the cow elk is about 30 percent smaller than the bull, her track is correspondingly smaller and thinner. The tracks of both sexes show up well in the dust of game trails, the muddy areas around wallows, and in light snow. The weight of the animal and its dignified gait make for a clean hoof imprint.

There are several types of elk spoor besides the tracks. The dung, unlike that of deer, is segmented in elliptical kernels. It is dark brown in color and is deposited in piles when the animal is standing, and strung out when it is walking. The dung is found mostly along game trails and in feeding areas.

At the ends of high canyons, where elk love to shade up in thick alder

In early fall bull elk remove velvet from their antlers by rubbing young conifers, thereby stripping them.

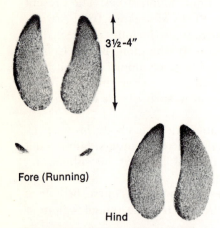

3½-4"

Fore (Running)

Hind

A heavy animal, the elk leaves tracks with clear impressions. The dewclaws register only in soft terrain and when the animal runs.

Elk dung consists of dark-brown kernels about an inch long.

and spruce copses, and where mountain springs have their source, elk make big wallows in the mud around the meager water. They roll in these, using the mud to rid themselves of insects and combat the heat. The water in the bottom of these wallows is a kind of time clock. If it is still muddy or roily, the animal that wallowed there did so recently. If the mud has settled, the elk may have been there several days before.

In early fall, the bulls rub and polish their great antlers to remove the summer velvet. They do this on young conifers, preferably fir trees. They choose trees generally at the end of high canyons or on the neighboring slopes, in places where they are unlikely to be molested. The velvet is rubbed off in a stripping action, with an upward sweep of the head against the tree. This, when repeated, also takes most of the bark off the young tree. The height at which this stripping occurs is an indication of the size and headgear of the bull.

Occasionally, in the fall, one will come upon patches of earth and grass which have been violently trampled and broken up. An area maybe 3 to 4 rods wide may look as though it had been rooted up by hogs. This is a place where two great bulls have done battle for a harem of cows. If the ground has been fairly recently disturbed, it will still have a faint odor at close range. This comes from the sweet, musky urine smell of the bull, which is pronounced during the rut. According to old mountain men, the mating bull elk is "the only animal alive that can drink a quart and urinate five gallons."

Once these various types of spoor have indicated the presence of elk in an area, and their probable numbers and whereabouts, several other factors can help to locate the animals. One is a knowledge of the times of day when the animals regularly feed and shade up. Elk emerge at dawn from the thick timber where they spend a great part of their time. Until about 9 o'clock in the morning, they will move about and feed in the open fringe and alps country between timber patches, and along open slopes, normally adjacent to the high ends of canyons. Between 9 and 10 A.M. they gradually work back into the timber, usually on the northern sides of the ridges, opposite to the sunny slopes on which they fed. Once in the shade, they move down into the thickest timber and brush patches of the upper canyon bottoms, which afford them protection against enemies, mainly man. Here any approaching enemy must of necessity cross brush, down timber, and other thick foliage, where his movement discloses his presence. At about 2 to 3 o'clock in the afternoon, the animals again begin to move and feed. During this afternoon period, and until the shadows have greatly lengthened, elk keep within the shaded protection of timber.

Once he understands such factors, the hunter then knows how to locate elk. The best procedure for him is to make camp at least a mile from where elk are expected or known to be. Then, before daylight, the hunter climbs the high ridges overlooking the great mountain basins where elk are found. He hunts for sight of the game as he moves noiselessly, without smoking, just inside the timber when he expects game to be in the open alps or in fringe country. The south slopes are the best places to watch at daybreak. If he sees no game going

During the day elk usually seek shade and thick brush that foils a stealthy approach by enemies. But if the sun isn't too hot, elk may lie in tall grass, leaving a bed like this.

A well-traveled trail through aspens may often lead to a congregating spot for elk.

upward, he then circles around the end of the canyon and comes back down the opposite ridge, still watching the southern slopes. At midday, it is possible to approach elk that are shaded up in heavy timber, but success is questionable. One must inch along noiselessly, into any breeze, and unseen. Even after such an approach, the old cow elk that habitually stands guard for an elk band on some vantage point will regularly see or smell the hunter, wheel away, and warn the others. The evening hours, again, are a good time to hunt, as the game once more moves and feeds in the open.

Horseback is the most productive way of locating elk. Far more ground can be covered this way than on foot. The procedure is the same — hunt early in the morning and as late as possible in the afternoon, concentrating on the high ridges and scouting all country below with binoculars as one moves along. If a violent rain storm breaks, it is as well to head the horses back toward camp. At such times elk huddle motionless in the thickest timber. However, just before a snowstorm, they are especially spooky and move about nervously. This is a good time to hunt them.

This species is migratory in that the animals move out of high country at least twenty-four hours ahead of a really big snowstorm and gradually head toward their winter ranges with that season's approach. In summer they may be high above the timberline at 10,000 to 11,000 feet, but in winter they move down to the less snowy 4,000- to 6,000-foot level.

During the normal September-October hunting season, a good elevation to look for elk is below the snow line left by a fall storm. And during this season, the very best way to locate the elk bands is with a good artificial elk bugle. The mating call of the bull elk is a squealing, whistling four-note arpeggio sounding like *Da-da-da-deeeee-da-da-dum!* In the stillness of a canyon this high-pitched call will carry for over a mile. With practice, it can be duplicated on an artificial bugle and is a direct challenge to the herd bull that made the real call to do battle with an intruding whipped bull with no harem of his own. Such a call should be bugled from the high ridges and canyon ends from which a real bull would call, at the appropriate time and at natural intervals. If the call is made realistically during the mating season, any bull within hearing will answer back.

After snowfalls, elk leave trails that are easily read. Many mixed tracks in a small area must be those of feeding or resting elk. Numerous tracks over the same trail (and a dozen elk can leave a trail looking like that of only three or four animals) indicate that the game is moving to another location. A single bull's track, widely spaced and going in a general direction, means a whipped bull, looking for another harem.

If a tracker is detected by a cow elk with calves, he will often hear a sharp yapping sound. This is the cow elk's warning to her young that danger is near. In early summer, when the cows play with their calves in the high alps country above the timberline, they make a gentler call to their offspring that is something like the distant peeping of seagulls.

11

Rocky Mountain Sheep

Many Sportsmen Consider the Rocky Mountain bighorn ram (*Ovis canadensis canadensis*) the top big-game trophy in North America. This is due not only to the majesty of the trophy or the palatability of the meat (a mountain sheep is the best wild-game meat of all) but above all to the real challenge that the species offers the hunter.

This species inhabits the highest, roughest mountain peaks and crags, in scattered areas of the West and Canada. Its range includes parts of such states as Idaho, Wyoming, Colorado, and Alberta and British Columbia. The original range once included areas of Oregon, Washington, Arizona, and New Mexico.

The Rocky Mountain sheep is a stocky animal of medium brown coloration. Big rams can weigh 300 pounds, but ewes are much smaller. Their outstanding feature is the massive curled horns which, in exceptional specimens, have a base circumference of 15 inches and a full curl measuring well over 40 inches. One of the features which can be spotted reasonably well at great distances with binoculars is the white rump, with its puny rope of near-black tail.

The general conformation of a ram's hoof is comparable to that of a mule deer, though a trifle shorter. This is misleading to the novice tracker. Under the impact of the ram's weight, the imprint of the toes splays out. The track, instead of being heart-shaped like a mule deer's, is blunter and almost rectangular in overall contour.

The dung of Rocky Mountain sheep is dark brown and generally kerneled (depending upon the food) but the kernels are matted together, as in the dung of domestic sheep. The dung may be found intermittently where sheep trails occur and in greatest abundance near the areas where the sheep bed down. These sheep beds are generally found in high open country above the timberline, on some rimrock bluff or bare ridge that commands a view in at least three directions. Sheep beds are nothing more than slight depressions in the shale surface. If the beds have been used

The dull-brown color of the bighorn blends with the rocky terrain, making the sheep tough to spot. But the white rump patch may catch the hunter's eye.

recently, fresh droppings in the immediate area will indicate the fact. This means that the sheep may still be on that particular mountain, or at least still in the region.

The best way to start hunting mountain sheep is with a fish- and game-map that is usually furnished by the fish and game department of the state or province in which the hunter is interested. Inquiries regarding the map should be addressed to the capital city of the relevant state or province. The map will show in detail not only the areas with sheep populations, indicating which are open to hunting, or only to photographing, but also the topography of the region and any roads or trails leading into it.

The next logical step is to contact a guide or outfitter. In some areas a guide is required by law for the nonresident hunter. In addition, his knowledge of the area and his equipment for getting to the game and bringing the trophy out of tough and often dangerous country are valuable to any hunter.

Hunting for this species is generally done from a base camp set in lower country, but reasonably close to the actual hunting area. Equipment can be brought in to such a camp and a day's hunting done from there. The hunter can then return to camp for a good night's rest unless he is caught out too late and has to "siwash." This means sleeping in what he has on and eating what he carries in his pockets, at the spot where he happens to be.

Horses are often used in this type of hunting. Sometimes the horses can be ridden up past the timberline, which usually occurs on this sheep's range between 10,000 and 11,000

The upper wall in this bedding spot provides the bighorn a convenient place to rub off shedding hair.

A ram may spar with a small pine, leaving this evidence.

Fore

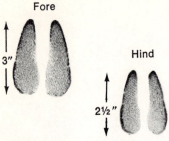

Hind

3"

2½"

Often mistaken for tracks of mule deer, the imprints of bighorns are generally shorter, with the toes set wider apart. Under the weight of a ram the toes splay out, leaving a rectangular print, distinct from the heart-shaped print of the mule deer.

Dung of the Rocky Mountain bighorn is dark brown, kerneled, and often matted like that from domestic sheep.

actual hunting only after game has been spotted in the mountaintop areas. There are good chances of such spotting, especially in the morning, and many hard miles can be saved if this is achieved before the game is actually stalked.

High-powered binoculars (8- or 9-power) are very useful for such spotting, but a still better instrument is the spotting scope, which most outfitters and serious hunters are rapidly adopting. This need not be a heavy glass. A scope such as the Bushnell Sentry, which weighs just over a pound and is slightly over a foot in length, is ideal. It can be easily carried on a packboard or in a saddlebag. Set on a tiny tripod that screws into it, it saves at least ninety percent of the hardest effort in finding Rocky Mountain sheep.

All areas of a mountain should be studied for sheep. The dull brown color of this species blends well with the rocks. Often one will look through the glasses right at a sheep and not recognize it as such unless it

feet, and then actually over the high, open ridges until game is spotted. More often that not, however, the horses are used to getting up the high valleys and as far as the timberline, and then the final hunting for sheep is done on foot. Sheep country is often "all-fours" terrain, and a person with good footgear can shinny up ledges, cliffs, and talus slides where no horse could go.

The basic way to hunt Rocky Mountain sheep is to find in advance a region where sheep are known or thought to be; establish a base camp in the general area; study all the surrounding peaks and crags from some high vantage point; and then do the

Horseback strategy. Using binoculars, hunters at 1 have spotted sheep at X. To avoid being seen, the hunters should proceed by horseback up the dry wash, using the trees as cover. At 2 they should angle downward through tree cover until reaching 3. There, shielded by the ridge, they can tie the horses and continue the stalk on foot. At 4, they may get a long-range shot at the sheep.

moves. Often, too, a ram will emerge from behind rocks, suddenly appearing where there was nothing in sight a moment before.

When you glass, good places to scrutinize are rimrocks overlooking a canyon; the area where talus breaks off from cliffs, affording the game easier passage; ridgetops where the sheep may be bedded down, only partially visible; any high, grassy benches among the craggy rocks; and areas of shade under cliffs, where the animals may be bedded down after the morning feeding. One should also watch the timberlines and the brushy vegetation just above them. Often, in years of drought, the high springs dry up, and the sheep move down toward the brush and timberline.

The game is seldom visible as a whole unless it happens to be glimpsed on top of a ridge, silhouetted against the sky. More usually one sees something which does not quite fit into the landscape and which, upon intense scrutiny, turns out to be part of an animal, or its complete contour. Two features of Rocky Mountain sheep are always easy to spot at great distances — their white rumps and the high-arching horns of great rams that form unnatural lines when viewed against a backdrop of mountain rocks.

If a large mountain cannot be glassed until midday or later, one may still elect to make the climb and look for game where it has shaded up just over the skyline to the north.

When working a mountain to locate the animals, the hunter has to be constantly cautious of being spotted himself. Rocky Mountain sheep have vision that is eight times superior to that of man. If a hunter comes within a sheep's range of vision, he will surely be spotted.

To a beginner, it might seem that an open sheep mountain, above the timberline, offers no means of concealment for the hunter. This is not true. Any mountain in sheep country has dips and gullies, ridges, and convolutions. Its surface is normally broken up by talus slides, tumbles of rocks, and at least some kind of short vegetation that can conceal the stalker. Often, when he has hunted for several miles over a reasonably open area where he has spotted sheep, they suddenly appear virtually from under his feet, where they have been hidden behind a pile of rocks or in an alpine gully.

The less abundant desert bighorn sheep, found in scattered areas in the Southwest and Old Mexico, are located in a similar way. The main difference is that in these desert regions jeeps and similar vehicles are used instead of horses for getting into the mountainous country and areas close to the scattered desert water holes, where the animals are most often found. When the terrain prohibits further travel with the vehicle, the hunting and stalking are done on foot.

12

Stone Sheep

THE STONE SHEEP *(Ovis dalli stonei)* is slightly smaller than the Rocky Mountain species and different in coloration. Adult rams weigh up to about 250 pounds. Instead of the roan-brown of the Rocky Mountain sheep, the Stone is an overall blue-gray color, with a light-colored head and a nearly black back. The adults' horns flare outward from the head and are relatively thin in diameter, compared with the massive, close-set horns of the bighorn.

The range of the Stone species extends roughly from Canada's Peace River country northward to the southern boundary of the Yukon. Some of the areas with the largest populations of this sheep, and the biggest heads, are the Cassiar Mountains in British Columbia and the vast area of mountainous country at the headwaters of the Prophet, Muskwa, and Toad rivers.

Stone-sheep tracks are similar to those made by Rocky Mountain bighorns, but a trifle smaller in size. In the light snow that occasionally occurs in early fall during the season when wild sheep are normally pursued, it is possible with any species of sheep to locate a track, and trail it to the animal that made it. This is, however, a poor method of approaching wild sheep. Their ranges are usually vast mountaintop areas above the timberline, where vegetation is sparse or nonexistent. Long before a hunter who is meticulously unraveling a sheep track can come close, the animal, with its marvelous vision, will have detected him. Generally it watches until it feels endangered, then retreats. A key secret in tracking or locating any species of wild mountain sheep is to remember that it habitually retreats from danger by going ever farther up the mountain, until it has reached the very top.

If the tracker suspects that he has been discovered, one procedure is then to circle around the entire mountain, climb to the top of it, and finally down on the game from the opposite direction. This often entails miles of walking and climbing. Another way, even when trailing in snow, is to de-

Here a large Stone ram beds within a cutbank. The sheep's predominant blue-gray color often blends with that of such bedding areas.

2¾"

Fore

2"

Hind

Stone sheep tracks are similar to those of the bighorn, but slightly smaller. Rather than attempting to follow the tracks, the hunter should use them as an indication of the presence of sheep and then begin slow, thorough glassing.

Stone sheep droppings are pellet-shaped and resemble those of the Rocky Mountain sheep.

termine the general direction that the animal is taking, then roughly parallel the tracks from far enough around the mountain so that its general curvature conceals the stalker from view. He must always, of course, plan his stalk so as to hunt into any breeze.

A good technique with Stone sheep is to trail not the animal but the trails. Old sheep trails are generally found at the timberline, well-worn through long annual use, often visible as they angle along the side of a steep mountain or work upward along the easiest routes.

In British Columbia there are big clay formations in certain sheep mountains, for example in the Prochniak Creek country northwest of Muncho Lake. In places, these big clay banks, sparsely covered with trees and vegetation, reach up from the creek beds near the foot of the mountain halfway to the timberline. Stone sheep regularly seek out these clay areas, where they eat the mud for its saline content. Sheep tracks made in these clay banks during the wet of early spring harden until they appear to be set in cement by fall. With the well-worn trails leading upward, they are a fine key to the location of the sheep bands.

During the summer months, the Stone sheep segregate according to sex. Older rams gather in large bands, leaving behind the lambs, ewes, and small rams. The sexes reunite only at the rut in the late fall. The occasional clear-cut sheep track found in the often meager dust of a sheep trail, can give the observant hunter a clue as to the sex of the animals he is likely to find on that particular mountain. Large, blunt tracks, measuring approximately 2¾ inches, are probably those of a ram. If the tracks are both large and numerous, they must have been made by a band of rams. If, on the other hand, the tracks include small 2-inch imprints, then the tracker is on a "ewe mountain."

The general tracking techniques are substantially the same for any species of North American wild sheep. Usually, the sheep are first spotted with high-powered glasses from a vantage point or from the valley below a likely sheep mountain; then the climb is made to them, keeping terrain, vegetation, differences in elevation, and the normal convolutions of high mountains between hunter and hunted so as to avoid detection.

In the past the problem of getting into good sheep country was as great as the problem of tracking and finding the game once one was there. The Stone-sheep range is remote and high. Roads over which vehicles may approach it tend to be sketchy, and the bush of the lower country is a real obstacle.

Once sheep hunters had to do much of their traveling on foot. They had to move to the base of sheep mountains, then make the climb and stalk. Often travel in canoes over the lakes of the lower country was used as a means of approach when feasible. Some of the Canadian hunters and their paying guests used big sled dogs in sheep hunting. A packsaddle with a pouch on either side, a bellyband, and a breast strap, was placed on a big dog. It was loaded with up to 40 pounds of rations and gear and was used all the way up a sheep mountain in the hunting of rams. A 90-pound husky dog could apparently carry such a pack all day without excessive tiring. Moreover, he could negotiate rougher terrain than a horse. With such a light outfit, the hunter could climb high into the alpine elevations of the sheep range, siwash out at night, and stay three or four days if necessary until he bagged his ram.

Horses are increasingly used in Stone-sheep country today. There is no better way to move personnel and gear from the end of vehicle transportation up the wooded valleys and creek bottoms to the base of sheep mountains. Planes are also used quite extensively to get into sheep country, but not for the actual hunting. Often these light planes are equipped with pontoons, and hunters are flown to the mountain lake nearest to sheep country. The hunters are set down, a camp is established, and all movement from there is made on shanks pony. Alternatively, the hunters may hike from the lake, with backpacks, to areas nearer the base of sheep mountains, and there make a temporary camp, sometimes within spotting-scope range of the game. Sometimes supplies are dropped at the spike camp with aircraft.

The best Stone-sheep country today lies just above prime grizzly country, so that the range of the two species often overlaps. It is very possible, when trailing or trying to locate one species, to come quite unexpectedly on the other. I found my biggest grizzly when two of us were scouting a sheep mountain for rams, and the monstrous 8-foot silvertip just happened to be digging for rodents in a high mountain meadow right below us.

At the northern periphery of the Stone-sheep range is another subspecies called the Fannin sheep *(Ovis fannini)*. This sheep has a nearly white head and a nearly black back and is locally called the saddleback sheep. It is thought to be a cross between the Stone and the Dall sheep. The techniques of tracking and locating this species are the same as for the Stone.

13

Dall Sheep

THE DALL SHEEP *(Ovis dalli dalli)* is the smallest of the major species of wild sheep in North America and one of the most beautiful of our big-game animals. It is one of the thin-horned sheep, pure white in color, and adults weigh 200 pounds on the average. An exceptional ram that I took in the Little Tok River region of Alaska some years back must have weighed considerably more. He had a 43-inch curl and annual horn rings that showed him to be nearly fifteen years old.

Dall sheep are found over a wide area of Alaska and the Yukon Territory in Canada. Like other species of sheep, the Dall is found in mountainous regions, generally above the timberline. Some of the areas that have produced numerous and outstanding specimens of rams are the Wrangell, Chugach, Kluane, and Tok River districts.

The tracks of the Dall species are almost indistinguishable from those made by Stone sheep, except that they are a trifle smaller in size. The tracks of ewes are proportionately smaller than those made by rams, as is the case in most species of wild game.

The basic methods and problems of finding this species are comparable to those involved in hunting the Rocky Mountain and Stone sheep, since the general terrain and conditions are similar. It is almost impossible to find a recent Dall's track upon some craggy mountaintop, and trail the spoor step by step to the sheep's location. The surface of sheep terrain consists of grasses, moss, and other short vegetation, and shaly rock. When hoofprints are made on such vegetation, it soon springs back into place, blotting out the tracks. Over shale talus slides the tracks show as a mild but detectable disturbance of the rocks. Where the shale is solid and unweathered, however, no imprints are left. Moreover, from the high open alps, slopes, and alpine saddles that they frequent, the sheep, with their vision eight times as keen as man's, are quick to spot the tracker. It is therefore far more productive to use any dung and tracks merely as an indication of the sheep's presence, and then to spot him visually.

The Dall sheep's white coat is easily mistaken for a patch of snow or ice.

Like other wildlife, the Dall sheep has been endowed by nature with protective coloration. Among the numerous small snow patches still remaining in the glacier elevations just under the highest peaks, his white coat is easily mistaken for patches of snow or ice. One can glass such an area carefully with the high-power binoculars, and often it is only when a white spot moves that it resolves itself into a sheep. In slightly lower country, against a backdrop of fog-drenched grass or the blue of great shale slides, the white of the sheep stands out in strong contrast. Or, etched against the sky on some high ridge, the Dall sheep is easily picked up with glasses, in part because of the break in the ridgetop contour.

When hunting this species with the visual spotting techniques, the hunter must first get to the base of the high sheep mountains. Then he proceeds to study everything on that mountain or range, until he spots the game. Using a light spotting scope with a 20- to 60-power eyepiece, it is possible to get a good look at game country, and often the game itself, for many miles around a vantage point. As an indication, the huge ram men-

Tracks of the Dall sheep are indistinguishable from the tracks of Stone sheep, except that they are generally smaller than those from Stones of the same sex and age.

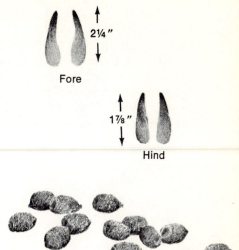

Fore

2¼"

Hind

1⅞"

The Dall sheep's pellet-shaped droppings are about ⅝ inch long.

tioned earlier was spotted from a ridge just above camp early in the morning, at an estimated distance of 7 miles. We stalked him all day, and finally got him about 4 o'clock in the afternoon.

On sheep mountains that have proven productive in the past, it is often worth climbing to the top even if no game can be spotted with the glasses from below. The ascent may take all day, with 20 miles or more of hard walking, but frequently the effort will pay off. The game may be concealed in one of the numerous gullies or at the head of a glacial creek bed, on cliffs or shelving ledges on the opposite side of the mountain, or behind some other form of barrier, and may be visible only from a position on the mountaintop.

Fog plays an important role in the locating of Dall sheep. During the fall when it is legal to pursue this species, mist, rain, and fog are common in high sheep country, especially in Alaska. A low mist or fog may blot out a whole sheep mountain for the entire day. If the day threatens to be foggy, it is best to stay in camp and wait for better weather. Occasionally, though, fog may be used to advantage if it appears when the hunter is already high up in sheep country. If he has spotted game in the open, and fog rolls in, he can often wait for it to move between himself and the game, then use this concealment to approach closer to the game.

In Alaska, horses are increasingly used both to approach the sheep ranges and, where feasible, to climb at least part way up to their extreme elevations. In both Alaska and Canada, light planes, too, are used to set down parties and gear on the high lakes closest to sheep ranges, from which foot-hunting may be done.

During the past few years, a form of bush tractor has been increasingly used for the same purpose. It is often of the caterpillar type, small in size but capable of pulling a heavy-duty trailer with a 1-ton capacity. At the tractor's front end a 6-foot blade is attached. The result is an odd-looking contraption, but the rig can easily cover muskeg, bogs often 3 feet deep, and the lush bush growth of the lower elevations. It simply plows through almost anything in its way when it goes overland or up the glacial creek beds that run high up into the sheep ranges. Small spruce trees and alders are pushed down by the blade and run over. Glacial creeks are forded with the tractor pulling the gear and people often loaded on top. Where deep cutbanks are encountered, they are quickly bladed into ramps that may be crossed. With the aid of bush tractors, many good, unexploited areas of Dall-sheep country have been opened up in Alaska in the past few decades.

14

Caribou

North American Caribou *(Rangifer tarandus)* are now considered to be one species. The subspecies of major interest to trackers and hunters are popularly known as Woodland, Mountain, Barren Ground, and Quebec-Labrador caribou.

The caribou has been driven by civilization northward out of all the lower forty-eight states, with the exception of a few animals remaining in the northern states adjacent to the Canadian boundary. But with the exception of the southern portions of Alberta, Saskatchewan, and Manitoba, the whole of Canada has a distribution of caribou, including the northern islands. The range extends through these to take in the southwest of Greenland. All of Alaska except the northern coast has a caribou distribution.

This species is an interesting one. The animals are midway in size between the mule deer and the elk, the bulls weighing up to 600 pounds. Both sexes are antlered, but the cows are smaller than the bulls. The caribou has a summer coat of a mousy brown. By late fall, the manes of the bulls have turned nearly pure white. The bulls' great antlers are perhaps the most striking feature of the caribou. They are massive in a large animal, usually palmate, with great upsweeping, basket-shaped beams and numerous tines.

One basic characteristic of this animal must be understood if one is to locate him with consistency. This is his instinctive compulsion for migration. In the summer the caribou herds move up to the northern tundra, remaining there for the calving season and for relief against heat and flies. In the autumn the food supply becomes unobtainable under a sheet of ice, and the herds migrate southward again.

During the last decades human intrusion has somewhat disrupted the animal's great mass movements. This has resulted in smaller herds that are more resident in nature. Yet even on their autumn ranges, during the period when man can legally pursue them, the caribou are still migratory in nature. A herd that is in a certain valley one day may be 60 miles away in another by the morrow. The animals' swinging trot can cover many miles in a short time, and caribou actually eat while moving along.

A good way to narrow down the areas where caribou may be found at a given time is to seek information from fish and game departments, outfitters, and local inhabitants. The areas where caribou come each autumn are determined to a great extent by topography. In late summer and fall, caribou love great rolling benches and mountaintops above the timberline, where they find both plentiful food and open country over which they can spot their principal enemy, the wolf. In both Canada and Alaska, these vast areas of high mountains, just under the peaks country of mountain sheep, are normally covered with large expanses of the ground-hugging caribou moss, other lichens, and the short blueberry bushes and arctic birch that often grow little more than knee-high. The alpine valleys and huge basins that often separate them are generally devoid of major timber, and the animals love to roam the undulating humps, buttes, high lakes, and heads of glacial creeks that are found in them. Visibility is often good for miles, and the food is abundant.

Normally, the caribou hunter has a guide or outfitter, who supplies the equipment and horses needed to reach the area and whose knowledge of the region is more extensive than the hunter's.

Because of the caribou's nomadic nature, one is never certain that the herds will be found in the same place from one year to the next. Moreover the presence of wolves in a valley will almost always mean that the caribou have been driven out, or thinned down, for that season. One factor, however, besides the general openness of the country they move over, aids greatly in finding the animals. They usually travel in bands and are therefore easier to track and to locate visually.

Once the hunter is in known caribou country, he should first take a stroll for a mile or so, up or down the glacial creek or stream which is certain to lie in the basin between the rolling, open hills that the caribou favor. If the animals have been recently in the area, their huge tracks are almost sure to appear along the watercourses. During the spring runoff, tons of glacial silt are regularly deposited among the glacial wash of rocks along the stream beds. When caribou work downward from one set of hills, they like to wander along the watercourses in the basin bottom before crossing over to the opposite hills. Their tracks will appear clean-cut somewhere in the silt.

The caribou's track is large in proportion to the animal's size and looks something like the imprint of a tiny round cushion. Within this nearly round contour, the hoof halves are widely separated, each being nearly crescent-shaped. An adult bull's track measures up to 4 or 4½ inches in length excluding the dewclaws and 7 inches or more including them. The imprint is splayed out and may reach 5 inches in width.

Unless left by a wandering bull at the beginning of the rut, a lone track is rarely found. By following the passage of tracks from one side of a creek bed to the other, one may usually determine where the animals have come from, how recently, and roughly where they are headed. It is almost useless

The caribou's white mane stands out against foliage or mountain backgrounds.

to try to overtake caribou on the move, as they travel along, even when feeding, faster than a man can walk. Morever, the resilient nature of caribou moss, blueberry bushes, lowbush cranberry bushes, and the other vegetation of the terrain they cross, causes their tracks to be quickly obliterated.

After the stroll down the stream bed, the next logical step is to climb to the top of a small butte or other elevation close to camp and study the entire valley or basin with highpower binoculars. 6- to 9-power is a good size, or, as with sheep, a small spotting scope is even better. From such an elevation, almost all the country for a mile or so in every direction may

The two varieties of lichens shown in the upper and lower portions of this drawing make up the bulk of the caribou's diet from the late summer into early autumn.

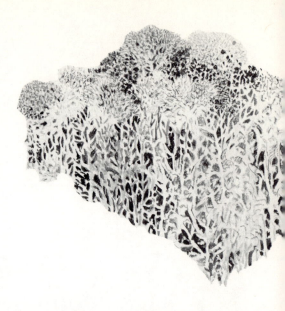

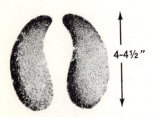

4-4½"

Fore

3½"-4"

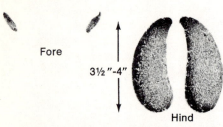

Hind

Tracks among the varieties of caribou are similar. The large crescent-shaped hoofs allow swift travel over tundra and snow.

Droppings tend to be bell-shaped and about ½ inch long.

be carefully scrutinized. This is the basic and most successful way of locating caribou. Often, under scrutiny, a distant patch of whitish caribou moss will turn into the stubby white tail of a bull caribou, or the top branches of an arctic birch will suddenly move, revealing themselves to be the tines of a bull caribou lying down.

Several peculiar aspects of this species aid greatly in spotting the animals anywhere in the open, even at great distances. The first is the white of the bulls' manes during the fall rut. This shows up clearly against either green foliage or bluish mountains, particularly as the animals are often in motion. A caribou also has an odd way of jumping high into the air whenever it breaks into its characteristic trot from a standing position. This movement, especially if accompanied by a glimpse of its white areas, is easily picked up with glasses. The peculiar leap is probably the animal's instinctive way of getting a better look over the low vegetation to see if whatever startled it is an enemy, especially a wolf.

This species is not wary in the way that grizzly bear, elk, or mountain sheep are distrustful of man. Indeed, in many cases it is downright curious and often mills about or stands and stares until a human presence is ascertained. With the onset of the rut in autumn, it seems to grow still less wary. The antics of the bull caribou, during the rut, appear to be sheer, purposeless insanity. For instance, a rutting bull may stand still and graze for a few seconds. Suddenly, for no apparent reason, he will break into a violent run, then after only four or five steps, he will plow to a stop and return to feeding. Or he may gore an imaginary bull or wheel in the opposite direction, stop as abruptly and start to doze. Such erratic antics can be picked up at great distances with binoculars or a spotting scope. Moreover, the general movement of the animals can be interpreted and a stalk planned that will bring the hunter close to them.

Caribou on the move cannot be overtaken, owing to the animal's speed and also because of the muskeg and soft mosses of the terrain. A half-mile trek over ankle-deep muskeg and caribou moss will exhaust a man who could run a mile or so without trouble. It is therefore better to try to determine where the animals are headed and then plan a strategy that will enable one to intercept their expected course of travel. Like other game, caribou normally lie down or rest within a small area during the heat of the day, and this fact is useful to anyone trying to come upon them.

Caribou in their usual types of ranges will amost always be located at a distance. Such country is normally full of knolls covered with blueberry bushes, cutbanks leading down to stream bottoms, and rolling benchlands. These facilitate the hunter's approach.

Occasionally, one will come suddenly upon caribou in plain sight and in the open. The best procedure in such cases is not to try to hide or move forward, and not to display any sudden interest in the animals or make any quick moves. If the tracker, without changing gait or staring at the animals, edges slowly away at an oblique angle until he gets out of sight, the animals are unlikely to move very far before calming down.

A useful trick in approaching a resting band of caribou in open country is for two men to crouch over together, tandem, just like two actors inside a horse skin, then angle slowly and obliquely toward the animals. The curious caribou probably mistaking them for a wolf, usually wait until they have approached to within long rifle range before bolting.

Field examples will illustrate how effective some of the above techniques are. A hunting companion of mine in Alaska killed his bull caribou not by chasing around the mountains after him, but by posting himself near his Indian guide on a high knoll, then eating his fill of blueberries. Several hours later the guide spotted game a mile away. A stalk was made and a bull taken. Another colleague strolled down a stream bed at midday, looking for tracks. As he watched, leaning against a pile of dry driftwood, he dozed off in the warm September sun. A huge pair of caribou bulls, moving up the stream course, nearly ran over him! My wife's Alaska caribou was taken after we had watched him at a distance doing crazy antics in a big open meadow. He would jump, run between trees, stop, swipe off a mouthful of grass, then jump again. Lastly, he bolted out into the open meadow, stood there a while, then went to sleep standing up. My wife shot him, after a stalk, as he stood there snoring. Lastly, by "playing wolf," a companion and I approached to within 196 steps of a small band of caribou containing a huge, white-maned bull with 54-inch antlers. His head now graces the trophy wall.

15

Antelope

THE AMERICAN ANTELOPE *(Antilocapra americana)* is the only prong-horned antelope in the world and is more of a goat than an antelope. Adult bucks can weigh 130 pounds or so, and the does around 70 pounds. The animals are a tan-buff color on the back and upper sides, with white lower sides and belly, a white rump, white bands around the neck, black face markings, and jet black horns on the bucks. Their dung is similar to that of a deer, but smaller.

The antelope's range runs from Canada southward well into Mexico, and from western Kansas to eastern California. States with the largest antelope populations are Wyoming, New Mexico, Montana, Texas, Idaho, South Dakota, and Oregon.

This is a low-elevation species. It inhabits desert flats, sagebrush lands, the rolling, treeless benchlands just above, and low, open mountains generally as far as such trees as the mountain mahogany. The vegetation in antelope country normally consists of short plants such as sagebrush, rabbit brush, cactus, and short grasses. Unless they are unduly disturbed, this is the type of country in which the animals will be found. One basic reason, besides food supply, is the fact that the coyote is the antelope's principal enemy, and in flat, open country antelope can see and escape him.

To narrow the search for pronghorns, one should hunt only this type of country. To narrow it still further, one should study fish and game department maps and management-area boundaries, and consult guides, local residents, and other hunters. The big ranchers in arid country are a good source of information and help. In many instances, antelope roam on their lands. Ranchers will often tell or show a responsible hunter where to find them, since the antelope may well compete with domestic stock for food. Sheep, for example, feed on many of the same short grasses, and cattle are grazed on the high antelope ranges. In these open expanses, there is often a visibility of several miles. The hunter's best tool is therefore a good pair of high-power binoculars.

Jeeps are often driven into good antelope flats, or the open hills just above, and the hunting is then done on foot. A careful study of antelope flats will always reveal depressions, gullies and washes, and occasionally green spots around a desert spring. These features are most useful to the hunter. The best technique is to move from the lower elevations, over which the vehicle has come, toward a higher basin rim, low butte, or other rises within the general area. As one moves along, he should look for the game and any tracks indicating its presence. If antelope are in the area, there will be tracks around any desert springs, any creek, or intermittently up the lower dry washes. Like many other species, antelope move down at night to drink where there is available water, then move upward with approaching daylight.

An antelope's tracks are somewhat similar to those of a deer, but straighter along their outside contours. An experienced tracker will not mistake them for those of deer, wild sheep, or domestic sheep. In addition to the difference in shape, their occurrence in flat desert land is a good indication that they are not those of deer or wild sheep, although antelope are often found in the same general country as domestic sheep. The front tracks of an adult buck run from 2 to 2½ inches in length. Smaller tracks indicate does, and significantly smaller ones, fawns. The fact that this species has no dewclaws can further help to distinguish its tracks from those of deer.

If tracks are found, they should be carefully studied to see in which direction they have moved up from any water hole or lower area. The next step is to move slowly to the top of any ridge, basin rim, or knoll in the vicinity. It is always possible, in antelope country, that the game may be just over the next rise. So as the hunter approaches the ridgetop or basin rim, he should just inch up the last few yards, then peer slowly over with only his head showing. Often antelope may be seen from such an elevation with the naked eye, but where this is not the case, the tracker should, from a sitting position, glass all the country within his range of vision with good 6- to 9-power binoculars. A sitting position not only helps to conceal him but is necessary for steadying high-powered glasses.

The best places to study in the basin ahead are the lower slopes, the area just under the crests of ridges, and the higher elevations. At dawn, antelope will normally be moving upward. Often, however, they cross gully bottoms to move to the other side of a basin, so the bottom country should be studied as well.

This species is not too hard to spot when its white-buff coloration is seen against gray or blue shales or purplish sagebrush, or when the animals are silhouetted as they walk along some distant ridge. Usually one spots them first not as antelope, but as a spot or spots of white. Careful study reveals the spot to be the contour of an animal.

When the sun comes up, another characteristic of the animal often gives away its location. The white hairs over its big rump are erectile. When an antelope wants to alert others in its band, it fans these long white hairs upward and outward into a huge horseshoe shape. This signal is also used to tell animals at extreme distances of the presence of the band. In bright sunlight, and in the clear air of the West, it can be spotted with the naked eye up to 2 miles away and is often the first thing one will see, while glassing a large, totally exposed band of antelope. Once spotted, the animals may then be stalked.

If one does not locate game from one basin rim, it is best to move on to another. Often while crossing the first basin or valley, the hunter may surprise game that has been hidden from his view on the ridge by gullies, side washes, or other features of the terrain. If he spooks antelope in a basin bottom, they will not stop until they reach the opposing basin rim.

Antelope can run at speeds of 60 miles an hour or more, but if only mildly startled, and if the hunter gives no visible indication of pursuit, a running band is not likely to exceed 40 miles an hour. The animals run tandem, with the does and young running ahead and the older, bigger bucks bringing up the rear.

When the animals reach the opposing rim of the basin or valley, unless obviously pursued, they habitually stop on the very last crest. There they turn their heads in the direction of the apparent danger and study it closely until identification is complete. The degree to which they have been startled determines how many seconds this characteristic pause lasts. The best thing for the hunter to do, after spooking antelope in a basin bottom, is to drop to a prone or sitting position behind a bush or any other available cover. His best chance is a standing shot from here, at the

An antelope "flashing" its rump hairs alerts others in the herd of danger. This warning can be seen up to two miles with the naked eye.

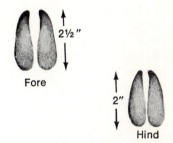

Fore 2½"

Hind 2"

Antelope tracks are similar to those of deer, but straighter along the outside contours. Since the animal has no dewclaws, tracks of like size showing dewclaws would be from deer.

When browsing on brush, the antelope produces pellet-like droppings about ¾ inch long. Grasses tend to make the dung a segmented mass.

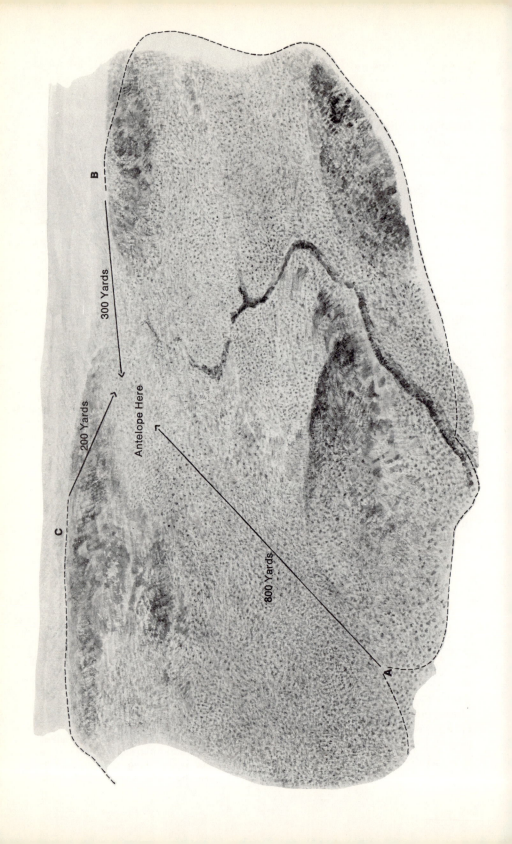

moment of that critical pause, rather than shooting, even several times, as the animals race away.

After the animals have satisfied themselves as to the extent and nature of the danger, they will move from the rim into the next basin, valley, or series of low-lying hills. The hunter should move after them, crossing the rim not on their tracks, but at a spot considerably to one side, where the animals do not expect him.

Often a hunter looking for antelope will come into flats or some great wide basin, and locate the animals as they are already looking at him. Antelope are comparable to mountain sheep in that their vision is eight times sharper than that of man. They do not necessarily break into a run, however, at sight of a distant hunter. Only when he betrays his intentions will they take off. If, on spotting the game, he makes no sudden movements that might reveal his interest, but continues casually along and then angles slowly off in another direction, the game is likely to continue staring at him until he gets out of sight. Once he has done so, by sauntering perhaps as much as a half-mile away from the animals, he utilizes any available cover to circle about and come upon the game from a different, unsuspected direction. In open country, this is the key technique for approaching any game that has spotted the hunter.

Like a caribou, an antelope is noted for his curiosity. In the early days many a hunter would lie low in the sagebrush of desert country, wave his red bandanna on a stick up in the air, and gradually lure the curious antelope into rifle range. Today's sophisticated game will not do this. But antelope do have an innate curiosity that will cause them to return, by a very circuitous route, to the general area where they have been startled, ostensibly to get a better look. Often they do so within a half-day. The patient hunter can often utilize this characteristic and let the antelope find *him* the second time. Moreover, when a hunter makes a siwash, or sketchy camp, overnight in antelope country, some of the curious animals will often be on adjacent ridges studying it when the hunter gets out of his sleeping bag at daybreak.

Strategy for antelope. The hunter must stalk antelope without being seen. In the drawing on the opposite page, the hunter at A spots antelope 800 yards away. He has two options. He can move behind the hills and high ground on his right to B for a 300-yard shot. Or he can stalk to the left (out of the picture), keeping lower than the line of sight to the game. He then crosses the crest of the large hill at far left and, at C, cracks down on the pronghorns from 200 yards.

In many areas of the West, outlying ranches that touch upon antelope country have alfalfa or other haylands. Antelope have a liking for alfalfa, and where their range is juxtaposed with this crop, they come at night to feed on it. Average fencing will not keep them out. Instead of simply jumping a fence as deer will, they travel along its length until they find the largest gap, then crawl under the lowest strand of barbed wire. Often the antelope hunter will find their tracks running along the outside of such fences. Moreover, at daybreak he may well find the animals still on the fringes of these outlying fields.

16

Rocky Mountain Goat

THE ROCKY MOUNTAIN GOAT *(Oreamnos montanus)* has a limited distribution. As his name suggests, he ranges only over this spine of country, in a thin strip extending from southern Alaska to the western states of Washington, Idaho, and Montana. His very limited habitat comprises the craggy peaks, cliffs, and shelving ledges around the tops of the highest mountains. These areas produce lichen, upon which the animal feeds. The craggy ledges and peaks of central Idaho, areas of the Bitter Root Mountains in western Montana, and regions of the highest, roughest country in western British Columbia, the Yukon, and Alaska are all typical goat country.

This animal is creamy white in color, with a long, shaggy coat that makes him appear to be loosely dressed in long woolen underwear. Both sexes have jet-black, spikelike horns that, in record specimens, measure up to a foot in length. The billies have pronounced humps at their shoulders, much like those of grizzly bear. Adults weigh up to 250 pounds.

As with Dall sheep, this goat's white coloration is a natural protection against enemies. Although both a Dall sheep and a Rocky Mountain goat will stand out clearly against blue cliffs or peaks, they appear to be snow patches. This illusion is fostered in the case of this phlegmatic goat by the fact that he moves about slowly and relatively little.

The mountain goat does not migrate very much. Occasionally, because of a limited food supply, he may change drainages. When he does so he heads down off the mountain peaks, goes directly across the valley below, then up to a new set of peaks. Usually, however, a goat seen on a certain mountain in the spring or summer is very likely to be in the same place in the fall—if the mountain is a large one.

This animal's tracks are sometimes found in the dirt patches caused by weathering along sheer cliff ledges. The front track of an adult billy can measure up to 2¾ inches in length. As in the case of several other species, the tracks resemble those of deer, except that the hoof halves splay out considerably under the pressure of the animal's weight.

The mountain goat limits his domain to the cliffs, craggy peaks, and shelving ledges near the tops of the highest mountains. The hunter should avoid a shot that will make the animal fall far and result in broken horns or a damaged cape.

The mountain goat is one species which is located almost entirely by eye. The peaks, cliffs, and lower talus slides of high goat country are normally open to view. In this setting the goat is visible, unless the observer is an amateur and dismisses the distant white speck as but a spot of snow.

Very few tracks of this species ever appear in the valleys and canyons below, so it is virtually impossible to come upon a fresh track and trail the animal down. The tracks are found only high up, after maybe a mile or so of climbing, in the animal's immediate vicinity. Once there, the hunter is likely to find tracks, but far more likely to spot the animal itself. For this purpose the best tool is a pair of good 6- to 8-power binoculars.

The best qualification any goat hunter can have is an ability to climb sheer cliffs, peaks, and rocky ledges. For this reason, anyone trying the sport should be in good physical shape and not beyond middle age. It is a thrilling but rugged endeavor.

After a goat is spotted high up in the crags, the pursuer should not attempt simply to climb up the face of the cliffs toward him, for two reasons. First, the undertaking is often physically impossible. Frequently goats are spotted as they feed along or peer down from ledges where a rock dislodged by them would fall vertically for several hundred feet. Secondly, it is best to hunt a Rocky Mountain goat from above, since his survival strategy is always to watch for any danger approaching from below. This is because no enemy lives above him, with the single and only partial exception of the golden eagle, which lives within his range. It takes many of the young kids but represents no real danger to the adult animals. An impressive indication of the height of a goat's habitat is the fact that a goat hunter will often see this eagle soaring downward over the canyon, below both himself and his quarry.

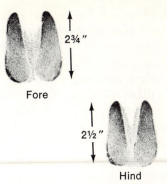

Fore

Hind

The tracks are found in dirt patches caused by weathering of cliffs.

Goat droppings are ⅝ inch in length and somewhat smaller than those of deer and sheep.

To reach a located goat, and relocate him after a stalk has been made, it is necessary to plan an approach strategy. Almost always, after a goat has been seen in the high cliffs, one can find a way to circle, go up some ridge to the very top of the mountain, then stalk down on the animal. This often entails hiking a mile in the bottom country, to where there is an ascending ridge that one can follow upward.

I have found 100 feet of light-but-strong nylon rope to be most valuable for climbing in goat country. Often there are areas of huge rocks, small chasms and cliff faces, and other places where footing is limited, but which can be crossed by hanging onto a length of stout rope. The hunter can, for example, let himself down over a 10-foot rock by anchoring a rope solidly to another smaller rock above it, then sliding down over the face of the rock using the rope to slow himself down. Conversely, he can often lasso the jutting top of a huge rock from below, and pull himself up over it. When going downward over such places, he should always cut off the rope leaving a section anchored in place, for his return.

After a hunter has made a climb and reached the cliffs where he previously spotted a goat, he will often find his first tracks again. In addition, any spare bushes along the very top may carry a few of the white hairs left by the animal as it moved about. Goat dung, too, may be found. This is dark in color and consists of individual kernels matted together in clumps, much like that of domestic sheep.

Once he is close to where the animal was last seen, the hunter should proceed very slowly and noiselessly. He should try, if at all possible, to approach upwind. A Rocky Mountain goat's hearing and vision are not as keen as a wild sheep's, but he has a good sense of smell.

Often a goat may be within a few rods of the hunter climbing down toward him, and yet not be seen because of intervening rocks, cliffs, or ridges. If the hunter feels that he is very near the unsuspecting animal, but patient scrutiny fails to reveal it, a productive stunt is to toss a small rock out into an open area and let it rattle downward. Often a goat that has been resting in a concealed place will grow curious and move out into the open to investigate.

Finally, it is always wiser, for safety reasons, for two hunters to hunt together for goats, instead of working the treacherous country alone.

17

Cougar

WITH THE EXCEPTION of the jaguar, the cougar *(Felis concolor)* is North America's largest cat. The animal is also known as the mountain lion and in the past was referred to as the puma or panther.

This graceful wild cat is tawny in color. The biggest toms weigh 200 pounds and over, and measure up to 8 feet in length, including the tail. At one time the species was quite widely spread over the United States, but distribution today is limited to west of the Mississippi. In a north-south direction, the cougar ranges from southern Canada down into Mexico. It likes the high rimrock country of such deer-populated areas as the Kaibab Forest and the breaks of the Salmon River Gorge in Idaho. In spite of its great strength, the animal is very shy of man, like the grizzly bear. It is nocturnal in nature, and avoids man by shading up in such inaccessible areas as the rimrock country of high basin rims.

Deer is the principal food of the cougar, though it will kill domestic stock, principally the young. It is very fond of young colts, and most horses, unless trained in the trailing of this big cat, will go wild at the smell of one.

Because deer constitutes their main diet, most cougar are found in scattered areas with big mule-deer concentrations. An adult cougar will kill up to 50 deer a year and can quickly dispatch a 300-pound mule-deer buck. It makes its kill by stalking the deer, then making a short rush, grasping the animal by the head or neck and sinking its fangs into the spinal cord at the neck.

Because of its innate wariness of man and its habit of shading up in the roughest of rock country during the day, a cougar is rarely seen by the average foot-hunter. Occasionally, a hunter after big mule-deer bucks may see a shadowy form moving swiftly among the rocks of some high basin rim, or slinking at dusk across some mountain road in front of his vehicle as he comes out of high country. But many hunters who spend their lives in the hills never get a glimpse of a live cougar, unless it is treed by dogs.

The cougar's track is nearly round in outline and measures from 3 to 3¼

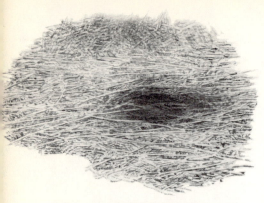

This is the "scratch" left behind by a cougar when covering dung or urine. The cougar will scratch the dirt backward with its hind feet in the direction he has come from.

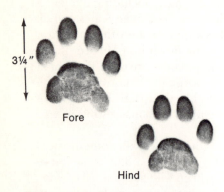

3¼"

Fore

Hind

The cougar's tracks are semicircular. The impressions left by the hind-feet are similar to those of the front, except that they are narrower.

Dung of the cougar tends to have deep constrictions, or it may be pellet-like. It often shows undigested hair, or even porcupine quills.

inches in width. In damp sand or dry dust, the toe marks show, but on most surfaces such as pine needles, ordinary dirt, or a skiff of dry snow, the track shows as just a round depression. In dry snow several inches deep, a cougar's track is diffused and looks something like the track of an elk in similar snow, where the hoof marks do not show. The stride is comparable, as is the width between the left and right tracks.

In snow, either wet or dry, it is possible to track a cougar for quite some distance, once it is picked up by the foot-hunter. But almost invariably the tracks will ultimately fade out or become most difficult to follow, as the animal meanders back and forth into cliff areas, patches of rocks where the snow has not stuck, or even across large logs that have fallen over mountain creeks.

More disconcerting to the foot-hunter is the fact that a cougar's course of travel is seldom predictable. He may wander in and about timber in a seemingly aimless fashion. He may decide to climb steeply out of a rocky gorge, move about for several hundred yards in top country, then as suddenly proceed steeply downward into the same gorge, on a course roughly parallel to the one by which he ascended.

The animal does, however, have one basic characteristic of movement. The old toms especially like to travel a large area in a wide circuitous route, much as a grizzly periodically covers his domain. In vast regions like the rimrock country of the Southwest, this route extends over many miles, and the animal will cover the route about every eleven days. In doing so, the cougar will make periodic trips into side canyons, but his general route is over the mountain saddles between the highest peaks. He leaves some kind of scent or spoor in his passing, and professional cougar hunters therefore like to work these high saddle areas with their dogs. If the cougar's passage, repeated every eleven days, has occurred within the past day, the dogs will pick up the scent. Otherwise, there is apt to be at least one telltale sign left by the passing animal. Like a domestic cat, the cougar periodically scratches the earth backward between his hind feet. This scratching sometimes serves to cover his excreta, but at other times seems to fill no purpose at all. It makes a dip in such surfaces as pine needles and dead leaves, to a depth of around an inch and over an area the size of a small plate. The wise cougar hunter will not only look for fresh scratchings but also bear in mind that a cougar will habitually pull the dirt in the direction from which he has come.

Such facts are not too important to the foot-hunter who can only find intermittent spoor, and who cannot hope to cover the same ground as a traveling cougar; but they are vital to the hunter who pursues cougar with dogs. This is the only satisfactory way of hunting this wary nocturnal animal. A good hunting dog will "read" the scent with his nose and if the track is reasonably fresh, can unravel it to where the cougar is. It can do so not only in snow, but over dirt, vegetation, rocks, and dry watercourses where a man sees no sign whatever.

Hound dogs are the basic breed used by cougar hunters. Good individual breeds are the Walker, Plott, Black and Tan, and often the bloodhound. Hunters like breeds and individual dogs that can be trained to ignore deer, bobcats, and other small game, and concentrate only on lion. They like hounds that will stay with a treed cougar for days if necessary, and in a large pack they like at least one dog with some bloodhound in him, for unraveling a "cold" trail.

Horses are used where possible, in conjunction with the dogs. The hunters ride, taking the dogs on leash over the general routes the cougar are known to travel, and proceeding until the dogs pick up a scent. If the hounds become excited, indicating by their actions and barking that the track is fresh, then they are turned loose. With luck, they will track the cat down, give it a short run as it breaks from the rocks, and send it up a tree that they cannot climb. They indicate the fact with a baying different from the type of barking that they use in trailing the animal. The hunters then follow up, often trekking laboriously for miles over the most inaccessible country, until they come upon the treed cougar, with the dogs waiting below.

Early morning is the best time for the dogs to get upon a fresh scent, since the dew holds the scent of the cougar well. After a half-day of hot sunshine, the scent burns out. Rain, too, quickly dissipates it.

Perhaps the best way for the average person to hunt or photograph a cougar is to team up with a professional cougar hunter who has a pack of trained cat dogs, then use his animals, his experience, and his knowledge of the tough cougar country.

In most western states the cougar has now been given the status of a game animal, where formerly he was regarded as but a predator. Seasons have been set as for other big game, and those who wish to hunt for this marvelous animal must do so within hunting-season limits. There are some exceptions, however. In certain areas, largely for the benefit of hound owners and nonhunters, cougar may be trailed and treed at other times of the year. But once treed, they may only be photographed or studied, not harvested.

18

Javelina

THE JAVELINA or collared peccary *(Pecari angulatus)* is one of our smallest big-game animals. This animal is often known as a wild pig, and it does have many porcine characteristics. It measures about 2 feet at the withers and nearly 3 feet in length. Average weight is from 30 to 50 pounds, with exceptional specimens reaching 60 pounds or over. The animal is blackish-gray in color and resembles a small pig with bristles. Its long snout has wicked tusks of considerable size, making it formidable against dogs, or when cornered or wounded by man.

Like those of many other species, the numbers of the javelina have diminished, and its current distribution is in the south of Arizona, New Mexico, Texas, and Mexico. The species covers a wide range of elevations, usually over arid country, from the Texas low country to mountainous elevations in Arizona of 6,000 feet and over.

A number of characteristics make the javelina somewhat easier to track and locate than certain other species of big game. First, the species travels in bands of up to several dozen animals in some instances. Secondly, if there is plentiful food and they are not unduly disturbed there, javelina tend to stay within a limited area. Such an area may hold a band of the animals all summer.

Another thing that often helps in locating the animal is its scent gland, located not on the legs as in the case of deer, but on the spine about 7 inches above the tail. This gland gives off a musky smell which can be smelled downwind for distances of nearly a hundred yards and which hovers above fresh feeding areas.

The animal's liking for prickly pear can be a further helpful factor. The bites it takes out of the spiny leaves will give an indication both of the freshness of spoor and of the possible numbers in the band. Moreover, like domestic hogs, javelina root in the ground for edible roots, and the freshness of these diggings will indicate how far ahead the slow-moving band may be, and again their probable numbers.

Recently browsed prickly pear is a sign that javelina are nearby.

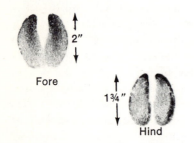

Fore

Hind

2"

1¾"

The javelina's walking tracks are usually staggered, with the hind foot falling behind and to the inside of the track left by the forefoot.

Javelina droppings are varied in form, depending on the animal's diet. They may be soft, and almost formless, or pellet-shaped.

Javelina tracks measure 2 inches or so in length, not counting the dewclaws, and resemble those of a small domestic hog. The dewclaws on the forefeet often show in sandy terrain. An unusual feature of the hind feet is that each has only a single dewclaw on the inside of the foot.

Javelina like hot, arid country with cactus and other low, sparse vegetation. In their movements in search of food they like to travel in dry washes. In the sandy soil usually found in these washes it is possible to track a band of javelina for considerable distances. If patiently unraveled, such tracks eventually lead to the animals themselves, or at least indicate the general area toward which they are headed. Like many other species of game, this animal likes to feed in the early morning, then lie down in the shade during the intense midday heat. Javelina are easier to see when standing, both in motion and stationary, than when lying down.

In the mountainous country of the Southwest, javelina are spotted visually. Where large tracts of country can be surveyed at one time, this is the best way. As with other species, one goes to a high spot, such as the rim of a basin or a butte in its center, then studies the entire area meticulously with binoculars. As with wild sheep, the scrutiny should be intense and complete. Often an animal or a group of animals that has been standing behind a clump of prickly pear will move out into the open after an hour's watching.

Texans have devised several ways of hunting javelina in country that is too thickly covered with high prickly pear to hunt successfully on foot. Ordinarily their hunting is done on the big private ranches. One way is to equip an open jeep with roll bars above the rear end. The driver then plows with the rugged little vehicle through thick stands of prickly pear often reaching nearly a man's height. Where the clumps cannot be avoided, they are simply run over and through, often with the big leaves breaking off and flying in all directions. One or two hunters stand in the back and try to hang on. If they can ride such a bucking mechanical broncho well into stands of pear known to have javelina workings, they can often spot the animals from their high position, as the animals stand or move between pear patches. Once an animal is spotted, a stalk is made. This is easier with javelina than with some species owing to the fact that they do not see too well, though they do have a keen sense of smell.

A variation on the above method of hunting involves the installation of a swivel chair on top of a jeep station wagon. A single hunter rides on this elevated chair, looking for the animals while the driver pushes the vehicle through negotiable brush and prickly-pear terrain. Often animals can be spotted from this high position when they can be seen in no other way.

A third method is to use the same type of high deer-stand that is used in similar brushy country in the hunting of whitetail deer. These stands take some time and effort to build and to move from one place to another, so they are generally set in known javelina country in the first place.

In the mountainous country of Arizona, in areas not containing many prickly-pear stands, javelina feed on the century plant. Where this plant is abundant and shows signs of javelina workings, the area should be carefully scouted. A basic rule in hunting this species is always to hunt upwind.

19

Bison

THE AMERICAN BISON *(Bison bison)* is a huge animal characterized by an enormous head, massive shoulders, short black horns in both sexes, shaggy brown-black hair, and a beard. Adult bulls can weigh over 2,000 pounds.

Approximately 30 percent of North America was once inhabited by bison, which roamed over the generally low grasslands from Canada's Peace River country to Mexico. The killing of the bison herds, generally approved by the government in order to make way for developing agriculture, is well-known to every student of history. The thousands of bison have been reduced from some time now to a relatively few, which today occupy three scattered areas. These are a small area in northern Alberta overlapping into the Northwest Territory; a second area including parts of Wyoming, Montana, and the North and South Dakotas; and a smaller third area in the Southwest at the New Mexico-Colorado-Kansas-Oklahoma-Texas junction. In addition, there are a few experimental plantings in other areas, including one in Alaska. Most of the remaining bison are now located in sanctuaries such as Yellowstone Park and on big ranches, most of them under federal or state supervision.

The bison has always been a romantic animal, possibly because of the era of Indian wars and western settlement with which the great herds were associated. But to most Americans, the bison has always been the "buffalo." At least one classic of western music has to do with the roaming of the western buffalo. And many a pioneer, in his rugged western trek, has cooked his bannock over a prairie fire consisting mostly of dried buffalo chips.

The tracks of the bison are something like those of an overgrown Hereford steer. They are round in contour with a moderate space between the hoof halves. The front tracks measure from 5 to 5½ inches, and the hind ones from 4 to 4½ inches. The bison is a good example of an animal with heavy front quarters that need more substantial hoofs, with a broader bearing surface, than the lighter hindquarters.

The dung of the bison is soft in nature, because of the normal diet of grasses, and resembles that of domestic cattle. Flattened by dropping and dried by age, it becomes the famed buffalo chips of western legend.

The hunting of this great animal is now a thing of the past. Occasionally a ranch or sanctuary herd will have to be reduced by the specially authorized killing of a few older animals, but this is a poor type of hunting.

Because of the bison's romantic past and to some extent because of his great size, most outdoorsmen are still attracted to him. The current interest is to see and photograph the animal in the sanctuaries where he is found. The usual procedure is simply to sneak up close enough to get a good picture.

It is possible to track bison in the sanctuaries or on the big ranches where limited numbers of the animals are still found. The big tracks can be easily read, in both snow and earth, in the meadows and grasslands where the bison graze. The big, flattish piles of dung also help in such tracking.

In most cases, however, the locating of a bison, or a small bison herd, is done entirely by eye. Once in country where bison are known to be, one simply moves through the area on foot or horseback until the animals are spotted. They habitually show up very well at great distances as huge blackish spots on the landscape. This is especially the case if they happen to be standing or even lying down in meadow- or grasslands, but even in sparse timber, they stand out well and are not usually mistaken for shadows.

There is one basic caution that the photographer should bear in mind

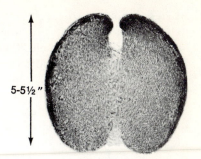

5-5½"

Fore

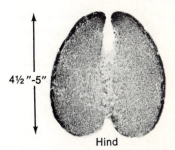

4½"-5"

Hind

Tracks of the bison are somewhat like those of an overgrown Hereford steer. But the forefeet, supporting the animal's great forward hulk, are considerably larger than the hind.

Bison dung is soft and resembles that of domestic cattle. Flattened and dried by age, it becomes the buffalo chip of American legend.

when sneaking up to get a good close-up of bison. The huge animals look to be entirely docile, but this appearance is deceptive. Bison have a nervous and uncertain temperament. Like some other species, they are pestered by insects in the summer months and often lie in low wallows until their great hides are caked with mud. This insulates them somewhat against flies and other insects. The craze of the rut affects them, too, as it does other wild beasts. A basic rule, therefore, when photographing bison is to do so with some climbable trees handy if possible. If the animals must be photographed in the open, then one should not approach too closely, but rely on telephoto lenses.

I once helped feed elk on winter feed grounds where there was also a small herd of bison. Big elk bulls would not go too close to the bison, even while feeding; and the horses pulling the hay sled could not be driven too near them, either. When an elk got too close, it was a revelation to see how the bison would wheel and make a dash for the smaller elk, with nearly the speed of a horse and the power of some animated bulldozer.

I have found while photographing bison in sanctuaries that the telltale sign of danger lies in the animal's short tail. When it comes up, letting the short tassel droop downward like an old-fashioned beet hoe, then it is high time to beat a hasty retreat from that general area.

PART TWO

SMALL GAME

20

Cottontail

Just as the Whitetail Deer is the all-American big-game species for many people, so the lowly cottontail *(Sylvilagus)* is our number one species of small game. Youths learn how to locate and hunt cottontails before they get experience with other species, and many oldsters, unable to stand the rigors of hunting for larger animals, end their sporting days with a cottontail hunt. One big reason is that, besides his sporting qualities, this small animal has such an extensive distribution and such an abundant population. Practically every one of the contiguous forty-eight states has cottontails, and in a north-south direction, they range from southern Canada through Mexico.

The cottontail weighs only 2 or 3 pounds and measures about a foot in length. He is grayish-brown in color, his most noticeable feature being the white undertail, which bobs up and down as he runs, giving him the name cottontail. The palatability of the animal's flesh provides an added attraction for hunters.

The cottontail's habitat is varied as well as extensive. The animal lives next door to civilization but likes the most brushy areas, as far removed from contact with man as possible. His favorite forms of cover include willow banks, cattail patches, thickets of wild rose bushes, fence lines, and any form of brier patch that will give him concealment from such enemies as foxes, hawks, owls, coyotes, and domestic cats. The cottontail's pattern of living is to find such an area of thick, protective brush and then radiate out from it into more open feeding areas, which usually include farmlands. The animal is particularly fond of clover.

Often faintly defined runways result from the numerous trips back and forth between cover and food. To locate cottontails, one of the first things to look for are these small trails leading out from thicket cover. If cottontails live there, one may be sure that their tracks will appear as a trail along the periphery of the thicket, with little branches running outward into more open areas.

The running cottontail's white under-tail shows prominently.

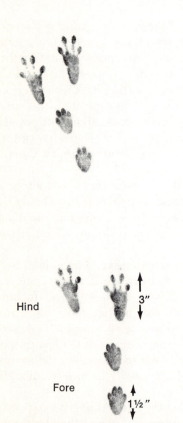

Hind

3"

Fore

1½ "

When the cottontail hops, its hind feet come down side-by-side ahead of the front feet. The distance between "hops" varies with speed and may range up to seven feet.

The hind tracks of the cottontail measure 3 inches or so in length, and the smaller front tracks about 1½ inches. Where the pattern of a hopping cottontail's tracks can be defined, the hind feet will appear opposite each other, with the front feet several inches behind, inside, and diagonally staggered. The distance between the imprints of the hind feet and forefeet depends upon the speed. A cottontail can hop along gently or break into a wild, zigzagging run. In light, fresh snow, his tracks show up plainly as pad prints, or oversized thumbprints in the case of the hind feet. In the dusty trails that the animal makes around thickets, individual tracks become obscured. The animal's dung consists of small, round, dark pellets.

There are two ways to locate this species, after having found the type of thickets and brier patches the animal uses. One is to foot-hunt the weed patches, willow banks, and brushy areas, mainly by first circling them and watching for sight of the animals around the outskirts. After a short feeding period a cottontail will return to the edge of his thicket home and stop for a time along the peripheral trail, generally on a slight elevation. Or, in the desert country that he often frequents, he will stop, after feeding, at the entrance to a lava-rock pile, into which he can run for shelter in case of sudden danger. He particularly likes to sun himself during these pauses. Consequently, the best areas to watch are the southeast edges of a thicket or rock patch during the morning hours, and the southwest fringes in the afternoon.

Often, too, one will interrupt the

The cottontail's dung consists of small, round, dark pellets.

animal as it feeds, sometimes a considerable distance from its home thicket. In winter, its gray fur is easy to see against the white snow, but among drab autumn weeds, it is not so readily spotted. Often the first thing one sees is a flash of gray, then the fast-repeated bobbing of the white tail, as the animal runs for shelter.

This little animal is like the larger antelope in one respect. Where the pronghorn normally pauses on the last crest before going out of sight into the next basin, the cottontail, unless too closely threatened, usually pauses for a few seconds as it reaches the beaten trail around its thicket, before darting inside.

Often a hunter may do a lot of walking around thickets and brush patches before spotting a cottontail, but this is a basic hunting technique, and the one most used by boys just learning to hunt this game little animal.

The second fundamental method of hunting cottontails is with a dog or dogs. Because the animal does not run long distances or go too far afield from the thickets he inhabits, a small, slow-moving dog is best for the purpose. The beagle is the preferred breed. In this form of hunting, most of the work is done by the dog. The owner simply takes his dog into the brushy areas known or thought to have cottontails and lets the dog do all the locating. Whether the cottontail is in the thicket or working the outlying fields for food, a dog with a good nose will pick up the scent and unravel it to the animal. Usually, there is a brief flurry of sounds in a willow bank or thicket, then a burst of bobbing cottontail emerging from the other side of the brush, with Rover in hot pursuit.

21

Jackrabbit

THERE ARE TWO MAJOR SPECIES of jackrabbit in North America. The blacktailed jackrabbit *(Lepus californicus)* is the smaller of the two, with a weight of 5 or 6 pounds. His habitat generally extends over the arid plains country of the West. The white-tailed jackrabbit *(Lepus townsendi)* is distinguished from the blacktail by his whitish sides, white tail, and somewhat larger size. His range covers the arid areas of the Southwest. Both species are actually hares rather than rabbits and have long ears and great running speed. Of the two the blacktail has the greater population and distribution.

The hind tracks of the jackrabbit measure up to 3 inches and the front imprints 1½ inches. The unusually long hind track comes from the fact that, in easy stride, the foot all the way up to the hock joint contacts the ground. The pattern of the tracks is something like that of the cottontail, though its grouping is longer. The hind feet leave imprints directly opposite each other, with the forefeet showing behind, somewhat inside the hind tracks and staggered.

On soil, rocks, or the faint trails found in areas with a large rabbit population, the tracks are ill-defined because of the animal's light weight and furred foot bottom. For this reason, it is virtually impossible to track a jackrabbit on an earth terrain. The task is easier on snow of any depth. The track patterns show up plainly, and it is possible, especially after a fresh snowfall, to track a jackrabbit down a fence row, ditch bank, or through sagebrush and weedy fields. The technique is to move slowly through the vegetation, watching up ahead, until the jackrabbit spooks out there. It will run farther before stopping than the cottontail, but still not beyond hunting range. At about 150 to 200 yards, it normally pauses for a few seconds and looks back. If it is still pursued, it hops for another short lap.

The tracking process described above is generally confused by the presence of other animals. The species likes, whenever possible, to live and feed in groups. For this reason, it is usually better to locate the tracks, then move through the area until the animal is visually spotted.

A better form of spoor than tracks will normally indicate the presence of the animals, especially in summer. This is their dung, which takes the form of small round balls, dark green in color, with segregated kernels measuring about ⅜ inch in diameter. Even on parched rocky ground in desert areas, if jackrabbits are or have been present in any abundance, the dung, even though old, will be there to bear witness to their presence.

In arid prickly-pear country, another form of evidence will show the presence of the jackrabbits, namely teeth marks where leaves have been eaten. During severe winters, when there is little other food, jackrabbits eat short prickly-pears down to the whitish roots.

The best general areas in which to find this species are the large stands of heavy sagebrush still remaining in some areas of the West, and around the peripheries of large stock ranches that border on extensive desert regions. The jackrabbit likes to feed on domestic crops, particularly alfalfa. Often it moves out into the desert areas by day, then at dusk gradually works in to the farmlands and raids the crops by night. In these locations, unless the rabbit cycle is at its lowest ebb, the animals are likely to be present by the dozens or even the hundreds.

This species has a cyclic population, the peak numbers occurring every seven to ten years. At the crest of the cycle, populations have often been so huge that agriculture in outlying areas has been threatened. In summer the animals eat the growing crops, and in winter hordes of them running into the thousands come in

After taking flight from the hunter, the jackrabbit will characteristically pause within rifle range to check whether he is being pursued.

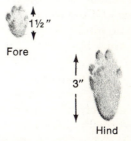

Fore 1½"

Hind 3"

The jackrabbit's hind track is much longer than the forefoot track.

Droppings take the form of small balls, dark green in color, measuring approximately ⅜ inch in diameter.

by night and devour alfalfa until large stacks are undermined and tip over. The Roberts-Mud Lake-Monteview section of southern Idaho is a region where such depredations have been an annual occurrence, and where some of the best jackrabbit hunting in the world is still to be found.

One good method of locating jackrabbits is to drive a jeep or four-wheel drive pickup around some of these large outlying ranches at dusk and watch ahead for the rabbits as they move toward the fields, from sagebrush or desert areas. Another possibility is simply to ask such a rancher where one may find "jacks." He will be happy to tell any responsible hunter whose aim is to reduce the population by a few animals.

Another good way to find jackrabbits is to drive a desert vehicle across desert and sagebrush areas, along one of the many old sheepherders' roads found there. Domestic sheep are summer-grazed all over the desert regions, and the tracks left by sheep wagons can be negotiated with a sturdy vehicle. In any area where a coyote is spotted, during such desert travel, there is likely to be a jackrabbit concentration. Jackrabbits are one of the favorite foods of the yodel-dog, who follows the big rabbit populations. Where an ordinary dog is not fast enough to catch the long-jumping jackrabbit, a pair of several coyotes will run one in relays until they tire him enough to catch him. Coyotes also dine off jacks killed by eagles.

The best time to locate jackrabbits is the early winter when they move in from the larger desert areas toward the cultivated fields. November, December, and January are the best months, since the snows are still shallow enough then to allow easy walking.

22

Snowshoe Rabbit

THE SNOWSHOE RABBIT *(Lepus americanus)* is actually one of the hare family. Indeed, his other name is the varying hare. The species has three unusual characteristics. First, the coat of this hare changes from gray-brown in summer to pure white, with the exception of dark eyes and ear tips, in winter. Secondly, the animal has oversized hind feet, which enable him to travel over the deep snows of his winter habitat without sinking in. Thirdly, the white winter coat, so well-adapted to camouflage against his enemies, is also exceptionally thick, thus insulating him against the frigid temperatures of the Far North, where he lives in winter without hibernating.

The snowshoe rabbit is medium in size, being midway between the cottontail and the desert jackrabbit. Adult animals weigh up to or slightly over 3 pounds.

The distribution of this species is generally over western Canada and Alaska, though the rabbit is found southward as far as the northern tier of states. I have seen it in such places as Idaho's Selway Forest. The overall range coincides generally with the conifer belt.

In summer, the snowshoe rabbit eats grass, any available clover, and other green plants. The main winter food, when deep snows cover all summer foods, is the northern willow. The rabbit eats the buds and bark of the willow, working the plants as the snows deepen.

In general, the animal likes willow and alder country, as well as the areas of scrub popple or aspen found on rolling hillsides, somewhat removed from the deepest bog and muskeg. I have seen the most animals in the region extending from Kluane Lake in the Yukon to Alaska's Copper River basin. The overall population varies, in part due to the cyclic nature of the species. During peak years, rabbits seem to be everywhere in the northern bush. In the low part of the cycle, the same areas appear to be almost empty of them.

There is a pronounced difference in size between the hind and fore tracks of the snowshoe rabbit. The front tracks measure up to 1½ inches,

The snowshoe rabbit's fur serves well as camouflage. Gray-brown in summer, it becomes snow-white in winter. With this camouflage, the snowshoe saves himself by sitting motionless.

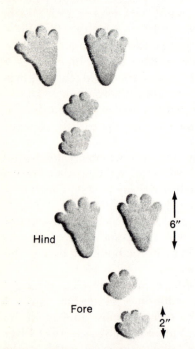

Hind

6"

Fore

2"

The snowshoe's running tracks show the hind feet registering in front of the fore. The wide snowshoe shape of the hind foot helps keep the rabbit on top of the snow. Winter runways are easy to spot.

but the hind tracks reach 3½ inches and truly look like miniature snowshoes, from which the name comes. On the summer growth of Alaskan moss, muskeg, and shale, the tracks leave little imprint and are virtually impossible to follow. The only way to locate the animals, without dogs, is to walk through areas of known food supply and spook them out. After a snowshoe rabbit is moved, it will not run as far without pausing as the jackrabbit. Unless pursued, it usually stops after 50 to 100 yards, and remains there as long as danger is present. Normally, where one animal is found, others will be nearby.

In late autumn, the gray-brown of the rabbit's summer coat is changing spottily into white. When the animal is scared up ahead of a hunter this pinto look makes it easy to see. In winter one has the advantage of being able to follow its tracks in the snow, but the rabbit, especially when immobile, is then very difficult to see, even from a distance of a few yards. The dark eyes and ear tips usually give the first indication of its presence. Then, upon close scrutiny, the form of a rabbit emerges.

In areas of known snowshoe-rabbit populations, the best way to locate the animals is simply to walk them up. In autumn this can be done along the numerous game trails, creek courses, and roads driven through the bush country by hunting parties and oil-exploration companies. Big-game hunters often run into areas where this rabbit is found and can then hunt it incidentally. In winter the best way to find snowshoe rabbits is the romantic, old-fashioned way of

Droppings are pellet-like balls about ⅜ inch in diameter.

traveling for miles through the coniferous woods and willow patches on snowshoes. Tracks on the surface of the snow will indicate the presence of game, its likely numbers, and the areas it is probably working.

Another less known species of hare is the arctic hare *(Lepus arcticus)*. This animal is far larger than the snowshoe rabbit, and much rarer. It is comparable, however, in that it inhabits the same northern areas and undergoes the same change in pelage — from gray-brown in summer to white, except for eyes and ear tips, in winter.

The arctic hare is the largest of the hare species, measuring up to 2 feet in length and weighing over 12 pounds. It is generally seen alone. Its tracks are proportionately larger than those of the snowshoe, but without the extreme difference in size between the hind feet and forefeet.

About the only way of successfully locating the arctic hare is to come upon its tracks in the snow, while hunting other game in its northern habitat, and then to scout the surrounding area. It likes the generally open areas in which it can run freely.

23

Gray Squirrel and Fox Squirrel

ONE OF OUR MOST DIMINUTIVE SPECIES of small game, and one that gives a lot of pleasure to hunters in many areas having few big-game animals, is the gray squirrel *(Sciurus carolinensis)*. This little fellow weighs up to 1 pound and measures around 19 inches in length, one third of which is tail. Its color is a mixture of white and black, giving an overall gray coloration.

The gray squirrel is widely distributed over the wooded areas of the East and South, and over southern Canada, generally in regions of hardwood and broad-leaved trees. The gray-squirrel population is not as large as it was decades ago, and the animals have an annual tendency to migrate between different areas, depending upon the quality and amount of the nut crop or mast.

The gray squirrel's hind tracks measure from 2½ to 2¾ inches, and those of the forefeet around 1½ inches. Both tracks have a decidedly bony look.

Like many of the small-game animals, a gray squirrel, because of its light weight, is virtually impossible to track for any distance over the leaves, grass, and other short ground cover normally found on forest floors. And, of course, the bark of trees where it spends much of its time shows no spoor. The basic way to find this animal is to go into a wooded area that is known or reputed to have produced squirrels in the past. Information from the local inhabitants or reports from other hunters are most valuable for narrowing down the areas to hunt. The actual locating of the animals then takes one of two forms—slow-stalking and still-hunting. Stalking involves moving quietly through the woods, watching for any movement along the ground, near tree boles, or in the branches of the trees. The stalking movement should be very slow, just an inching along. Any fast movement, especially toward an animal, will cause it to hurry away or hide. Today's squirrels are much warier than their forebears.

As the hunter goes quietly through the woods, his study of everything around him should be thorough. A gray squirrel is small, and when only a portion of its body in a treetop is open to view, it is often overlooked. An ability to interpret small spots and shapes in wooded country is most useful in looking for squirrels and can be developed with experience. It consists largely in looking intently, mainly into the branches.

Slow-stalking is called still-hunting by many hunters, though still-hunting in its strictest sense means to hunt without movement or sound. That is to say, one gets into a comfortable position, often standing or preferably sitting against a tree, in an area where game is expected to be. While in this "still" position, one should not make any sounds, smoke, or change positions. A slight sound or movement will prevent the game from showing itself or working in the trees. Often the person still-hunting in this way will become painfully cramped all over, but to be successful, he must endure the discomfort. In either type of hunting, it is best to wear camouflage clothing, which makes the motionless hunter practically invisible.

With experience, one comes to recognize two valuable indications of the presence of squirrels. One is the mild rustling sound the animal makes as it moves and works for food. This, with practice, can be distinguished from the sound of breezes and birds, and other normal forest noises. The second telltale indication is a basic form of spoor—the numerous cuttings or residue from the squirrel's nut supply. Abundant or recent cuttings mean that squirrels are nearby.

The best time to hunt the gray squirrel is at sun-up, or just after. A less productive time is sunset. During

Squirrels sometimes build leaf nests, which may be cooler than tree hollows in the summer but offer less protection from the elements or predators.

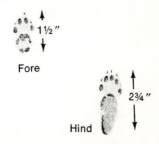

Tracks of both the gray and fox squirrel have a bony appearance.

Squirrel droppings like these may be harder to locate than chewed or "cut" nutshells, which provide sure evidence of squirrels.

these two periods of the day squirrels do most of their moving about. During the heat of day, they like to shade up, usually in their treetop leaf-shelters. Like other game species, with the exception of waterfowl, squirrels do not like to move about in rain or wind but stay huddled in the leafy shelters and canopies.

Closely allied to the gray squirrel is another much larger species, the fox squirrel *(Sciurus niger)*. Adults of this species weigh up to 2½ pounds and measure about 2 feet in length. The fox squirrel has a gray back like the gray squirrel, but its belly, face, paws, and tail have a reddish hue, from which its name derives.

The fox squirrel likes less dense wooded areas, particularly those fringing on agricultural lands. Occasionally the ranges of the two species overlap.

The tracks and cuttings of the fox squirrel are similar to those of the gray squirrel. The methods of locating the two species are comparable. In addition, hunters occasionally elect to work with a dog that finds the animals along the ground and then runs them up trees. Terriers, beagles, mongrel house dogs, and other small breeds are used for the purpose. The best time to locate tree squirrels with a dog is during the late fall when a large part of the nut crop is on the forest floor.

24

Opossum

THE OPOSSUM *(Didelphis virginiana),* or possum as it is popularly called, is a relic from an earlier historical period. In appearance, this homely animal looks something like a cross between an overgrown mouse and a fluffy muskrat. It has a long, pointed snout, a hairless, scaly tail, and shaggy hair that is creamy tan-white in color.

An adult animal weighs about 9 pounds and measures up to 2½ feet in length. Over one third of this length is accounted for by the tail, which the opossum uses for climbing and hanging from tree limbs. It is one of our few marsupials, or pouched species.

In legend and song, this animal has always been associated with the South, possibly because it has been used there so generally for pot meat. However, its distribution is wide. Nearly every one of the contiguous forty-eight states has a possum population, though in some northern states this population is meager. The animal's range extends into southern Canada.

The opossum leaves an interesting track. The five bare, "knuckly" toes of the front foot leave spots in the imprint, instead of a complete foot track. There are only four toes on the hind feet. The equivalent of the first finger is a stumpy, clawless thumb, which points sharply inward in the imprint. The hind tracks of an adult opossum measure about 1¾ inches in length, and the front tracks around 1½ inches. The opossum's gait is waddly, something like the walk of the porcupine.

Generally, the opossum likes wastelands, including swamp areas, patches of sparse brush and short trees, the corn patches of agricultural country when available, and creek bottoms in fallow country. It eats berries, nuts, fruits, and insects.

The animal is nocturnal and does most of its traveling over short distances in search of food. For this reason, tracks are often seen in a particular area, but one seldom sees the animal itself. More often than not, recent tracks along creek bottoms, where cornfields border on brushy lands, and in dirt patches among sparse trees and low brush, will end at some hollow log

When pursued by dogs, the nocturnal opossum heads for the nearest tree.

1½"

Fore

1¾"

Hind

The opossum's front toes spread into a sparse, star-shaped track. The hind print shows an opposable toe.

Since the possum's digestive tract is very complete, the animal's scat is rarely seen.

or tree or at a rock heap, where the animal has holed up for the day. Frequently, however, the approach to these dens is over ground cover such as leaves, rocks, and short brush. This makes tracking the animal to dens, in daylight, most difficult.

The opossum can be successfully tracked only with dogs, and at night. The procedure, briefly, is to take a dog or dogs into the wastelands and brushy areas where tracks have been located, then let Rover sniff him out and send him up a tree. The hunter, meanwhile, goes along with the aid of a good flashlight, listening to the dogs, and eventually comes up to where the opossum has been treed.

Almost any dog that likes to hunt will follow scent and tree an opossum. Good coon hounds are preferable, but innumerable animals are treed by youngsters following along after their farm mongrels. The intelligence of the opossum is comparatively low, and the race he gives pursuing dogs is neither cunning nor long. As soon as the animal detects that he is being chased, he goes up the nearest tree, and the dogs bark "treed."

This lowly animal has been hunted extensively for pot meat and its cheap fur. Only its prolific nature, its ability to live in wastelands and eat almost anything, and the fact that it holes up by day and therefore cannot then be hunted well, have allowed its numbers to be maintained.

25

Raccoon

THE RACCOON *(Procyon lotor lotor)* is a bushy, low-slung animal averaging 15 to 20 pounds in weight, though exceptional specimens can weigh much more. Its color varies from gray-black to yellow-gray, with darker guard hairs and an overall grizzled appearance. The face is generally lighter in color than the body, and a principal feature is the black villain's mask across the eyes and face. Another distinguishing feature is the brushy tail ringed with black, which gives the animal its nickname of "ring-tail."

The great majority of raccoons was once found in the East and South, but as in the case of the opossum, a gradual migration took place westward, and northward as far as Canada. A sample of the westward movement was noted recently in our little town in eastern Idaho. Ninety-nine percent of the people living here had never seen a raccoon. One night late last fall one of the residents heard his family dog barking violently outside. He got out of bed to find that it had chased a full-grown raccoon from where it had been working in the sweet corn of his garden up into a shade tree above his house.

This animal's front tracks resemble the imprints of a man's hand in miniature, and the hind tracks, those of a man's foot, scaled down, with broken arches and flat feet. The toes, in each case, look long and skinny, and all have clawmarks at their extremities. The raccoon's feet are naked of hair. The front track measures 2½ inches or more in overall length, and the hind track from 3½ to 4 inches.

The raccoon likes wooded areas, especially those crossed by creeks or streams, on the fringe of agricultural lands. Traditionally, his home is a hollow tree or log, though he also holes up in rocky dens or cliffs. His food is that found in such a habitat, ranging widely from frogs, crayfish, grasshoppers, and nuts to fruits and domestic corn.

Consequently, the best places to look for this animal's tracks are those where it gets its food. It especially likes crayfish, and in creeks in coon country its tracks are likely to show in the mud or dirt along the banks. This

Raccoon tracks are often found along stream banks, like this and near cornfields, orchards, and garbage.

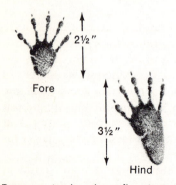

Fore

2½"

3½"

Hind

Raccoon tracks show five toes in each foot. On the forefoot the toes are as long as the pads but on the hind foot the pad is much longer.

Typical raccoon droppings do not taper at the ends.

trail is often segmented, since the animal may walk along for a short distance, then wade in the shallows, turning over rocks in search of crayfish, then emerge to walk along the bank again. Similarly, areas around cornfields in raccoon country will show the tracks, particularly where the fields border on woods. Once found, a ripe cornfield will attract repeated visits, and along the animals' more or less defined routes from the field to the woods the greatest number of tracks will be found. Old abandoned farms and outlying orchards are also good places to look for raccoon tracks. The animal, during fruit season, regularly comes to these places to gather up the windfall apples and other fruit.

The presence of tracks, however, does not mean that one can pick up the spoor and trail the animal down, as can be done with some big-game species. A raccoon is nocturnal and rarely shows himself during the day. Occasionally, one will see an animal at dawn, as it heads from its night feeding back into the woods, or toward dusk, as it heads into a creek bed. But generally, locating raccoons is a nocturnal undertaking.

One way to locate raccoons in a large area is to take repeated drives around the wooded back roads an hour or so after dark. Often a raccoon will be caught in the headlights of a vehicle, as it crosses such a road. I once traveled a road in the hill country of Texas where I saw several of the squat animals in this way, as well as a few that had been hit and killed by other automobiles.

As in the case of the lowly opossum, the only successful way of hunting raccoons is with dogs. Good coon dogs can pick up the body scent of the animal long after it has been in a certain area and trail it to where it can be treed. Every breed of dog is able to chase coons, but developing a good strain of coon dogs is an art. Many hunters like such hounds as the Walker, Bluetick, Redbone, Black and Tan, and Plott. Men who breed dogs for the purpose of running coons will already, in the dogs' training, have located the best local areas for finding the animals. The average person, without dogs, can often best find his raccoons by teaming up with a hound owner. Often the beginner, who buys one dog for coon hunting, can add his animal to the pack of an experienced dog owner and so let the young dog learn something of the art.

Because of the canniness of the raccoon, night chasing can be a wildly exciting sport. The hounds or dogs are usually trailer-hauled to the general area and then taken on leash to the spots where coons are known or thought to be. They are then turned loose to pick up any scent. The hunters try to follow, using electric lanterns and flashlights.

Once the dogs strike a scent, anything can happen and usually does. The raccoon, once alerted, takes off toward his woods den, with the hounds in hot pursuit. Some owners like hounds that will follow a scent silently, baying only when the quarry is treed. Others prefer dogs that bay all the way, claiming that this makes the chase far easier to follow.

The startled raccoon has a vast bag of tricks to elude the dogs. He may run a certain distance, then double back at an acute angle. He may twist back and forth in zigzag fashion, then break into a totally new direction. If any water is in the area, he is almost certain to make for it. He will swim the larger creeks, maybe run along the shallows on the far side, then make off into the woods, or double back, recross the river, and head back toward the area he left, while the dogs try to unravel his trail. Often after the animal is treed, he will wait in the treetop until the dogs are convinced they have him, then jump 40 feet downward away from the tree trunk, and strike off again. Add the blackness of a pitch-dark night to all this, accompanied by the frenzied baying of excited hounds, and the scene is of exhilarating but mad confusion.

A coon hunter should be prepared for such a wild outing. His clothes should be such as to withstand a maze of briers and branches, tough going over rocks and brush, and a likely wade across some creek. Also, he should be in good physical shape.

Once a raccoon is treed, the tendency today is to let him go, to provide further sport some other night. The thrill of the chase is considered far more important than the value of his pelt as a Davy Crockett hat.

26

Red Fox

THE RED FOX *(Vulpes fulva)* has been made famous in legend and children's literature, largely because of his ability to match wits with man and other creatures of the forest.

This animal is sleek and distinctive in appearance, with reddish yellow fur, a pointed nose, slanting, wise-looking eyes, a dainty body, and a long, flowing tail or brush. This tail is longer in the fox's northern habitat, where the animal uses it as insulation against severe cold by curling it around its body while resting. The fox's average weight is about 10 pounds, and its body, including the tail, measures about 3 feet in length.

The habitat of this species is extensive, covering large forested areas across most of the United States and from the Arctic to Mexico. The red fox likes regions that are sparsely timbered, often interspersed with grasslands, meadows, and fringe country.

The tracks of the red fox are somewhat like those of a small dog. The overall contour, especially that of the forefoot, is nearly round. In dust, where the track can be clearly identified, the small pad marks of the four toes, the claws, and the heel more or less enclose the imprint left by the base of the foot. But in fresh snow, the imprint looks like a single small, roundish impression. The tracks of the adult fox measure 2 to 2¼ inches in length.

Because of the lightness of the animal and the ground cover he traverses, it is impossible to track a red fox for any distance without snow. His tracks may be visible in the dirt of a trail for a distance, or where he crosses soft earth, but then they disappear as he moves off over grass, leaves, or weeds. On light, new snow, however, it is easy to follow the tracks of a fox. As with many other species, it is best not to trail directly upon fresh tracks, but to parallel them somewhat to one side. A hunter working with or without a small dog can often "jump" a fox he has overtaken in this way, generally as the animal is resting at midday.

The red fox, like so many other woods creatures, loves the dawn and dusk periods to move about for food. He also likes large areas of meadowland interspersed with timber, where he can work out in the open after rodents but have the protection of handy timber for flight from dogs and man. Watching such open meadows, or domestic pastures fringed with timber, at dawn and dusk is another way to locate a red fox. In fact the last red fox I saw was about 200 yards from where I now sit in my home office on our Idaho acreage. At dusk one night, he came from the woodlot and began cautiously digging in the alfalfa field for the mice that were infesting the area.

In Alaska, a good place to look for red foxes is along the coast, where they come to beachcomb for mussels and other food at all hours of the day. The cunning and general elusiveness of the red fox are legendary, but in several areas along the Alaskan coast, red- and cross-foxes (a cross between the red and silver varieties) have observed me at short distances without apparent fear. Off a Kodiak Island bay, a red fox once wandered up to within 20 feet of me as I stood stock-still against a cutbank just off the beach. Again, another of this species played hide-and-seek with me as I tried for a close-up picture in a grassy meadow just off Herendeen Bay on the Alaska Peninsula. I could get to within 20 yards before he would move away, and if I stood still, he would inch up within about that distance of me. These were foxes that had had no previous contact with man.

Over the many years of hunting the American red fox, two basic methods proved most successful. In the South and East, foxes were run

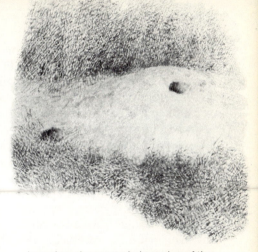

In spring, the most obvious sign of the red fox is a den, usually modified from a woodchuck burrow. The den is used only long enough to bear and rear the kits.

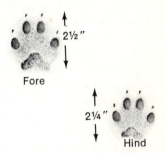

The red fox leaves a nearly round print, like the track of a small dog. In soft mud or dust the toe claws and heel enclose the pad imprint. In winter, fur grows over the pads and results in a less defined imprint.

Typical red fox scat is sharply tapered on each end and contains mostly hair and feathers.

by hounds. Hunting clubs were formed, dog packs bred and kept for the purpose, large areas of lands leased for the hunting rights, and fox hunting became a great sport of the elite. With this type of hunting, the riders and hounds were assembled at a given place. The party and hounds on leash were taken to a likely area and the hounds turned loose. When the hounds struck scent, the chase was on, usually over all types of open country and forested terrain. It came to be traditional, after the fox was brought to bay, that the hunters came up and instead of killing the fox, turned it loose to run again. This was in self-interest, since such hunts normally produced more exercise than foxes, and there was no sense in killing the provider of the sport.

A comparable form of fox hunting was developed in the northern states, the principal difference being that the hunting was done on foot, because the northern forest terrain was unsuitable for horse coursing. Several hunters, with their combined pack of hounds, would move by vehicle to a generally suitable area. The hounds would then be taken on leash to where foxes were known or reputed to be and there turned loose. They would cast about the area until a fox was located, then tear in after him, baying to advertise the fact to the waiting hunters. Meanwhile, the hunters separated and moved to the known fox crossings and runways. Often the hounds would run the fox in a more or less circuitous course to one of these likely locations, where the hunter would get his chance at it.

Frequently this method was successful. It came to be a game of wits as to where the hunters *thought* the animal would run, and where the fox elected to take the chase. Specialized hounds were needed for this type of chasing. They had to be tireless, give voice as they ran, and bark "treed" when the fox was brought to bay. Many kinds of hounds were and still are used for this kind of fox hunt. The two most highly developed American foxhounds are the Walker and the Triggs.

In the past few decades, the technique of having the quarry come to the hunter instead of the other way around has been highly developed. When calling a fox, the hunter, wearing camouflage clothing, hides in a suitable place in a known fox area and calls to the distant animal on an artificial animal call. The most effective call is the simulated squeal of a dying rabbit. When the call is produced realistically, at proper intervals and decreasing in volume and agitation to suggest a dying animal, the fox listening at a distance is irresistibly attracted. He comes cautiously but surely up to the waiting hunter, often to within a distance of a few yards.

27

Gray Fox

ANOTHER NORTH AMERICAN FOX with a considerable population is the gray fox *(Urocyon cinereoargenteus)*. His general distribution covers approximately half the area of that of the red fox, with the ranges of the two species overlapping in many regions. The gray fox is most commonly found east of the Mississippi, in the Northeast.

In many respects, the gray fox resembles the red fox. It has a similar slim form, pointed nose and ears, and a long, brushy tail. As the name suggests, its color is a grizzled gray on the sides and back, with buff underhairs. The underparts are light gray, and the tail tip is dark gray. In general, the gray fox weighs less than the red species, the adult's weight being around 8 pounds.

The tracks of the gray fox resemble those of the red fox, except that they are a trifle smaller. The hind track of the gray species measures from $1\frac{7}{8}$ inches to 2 inches. Front tracks measure up to $2\frac{1}{8}$ inches. Another slight difference is that the imprints left by the toe pads of the gray fox are somewhat larger than those left by the red fox, despite the lesser size of the imprint as a whole.

In general, the methods of locating the gray species are the same as those used in finding red foxes. It is impossible, except in snow, to trail either species. Both foxes are found by searching those areas which they habitually frequent; by coming upon them incidentally while in pursuit of other game or another outdoor activity; by the use of hunting hounds trained for the purpose; and, recently, by the art of varmint calling.

There is one difference, when coursing the animal with hounds. When pursued by dogs, the gray fox can and often does climb trees to elude his enemies. This frequently changes the pattern of the hunt and adds to the dogs' confusion. In coursing either gray or red foxes, dogs may well get lost, and in some cases, what began as a fox hunt turns into a hunt for the dogs.

Both species will come to the offal left by game kills and to carrion. Where, for example, there are intestines left from the dressing of a deer

The gray fox can climb trees to check hunting areas or to escape enemies.

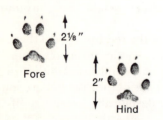

2⅛ "

Fore

2"

Hind

Though the gray fox's tracks are generally smaller than those of the red, its toe prints are slightly larger.

2½ "→

Often found along road edges or trails, scat of the gray fox is sharply tapered and usually contains feathers or the fur of small mammals. Since the gray fox eats more berries than the red, the gray's scat is usually darker.

foxes will come at first light to clean up the remains. These are good areas to observe repeatedly from a distance.

In brushy country especially, the gray fox is susceptible to varmint calling. The same technique as that used for red foxes is employed, and night calling is often productive. For this, one should choose a windless night, when sounds carry far. Moreover, the technique works better in open areas, devoid of large trees. Of course, areas with known rodent populations and other fox foods such as juniper berries are apt to yield better results.

The technique involves two or more hunters working together. First they drive, as noiselessly as possible, into the chosen area after dark, walking the last lap where necessary. Once there, the hunters get settled, generally low to the ground and sitting comfortably. Once the calling begins, there should be no further noise or movement. The caller begins with the loud, weird cry of a rabbit that has been caught. This call is repeated in sequences in the manner of a real rabbit. Then one or two lesser cries are made, followed by more loud squeals of fright.

After a few moments, during which any wandering fox within a half-mile should have been able to hear the sound, a second person begins working with a high-powered headlight. This beam, in the total darkness, is swept in a large but slow-moving arc, so that its rays pick up any movement in the distant brush. The procedure is continued for fifteen or twenty minutes, during which time any fox within the immediate area will have come to the sounds of distress. As he cautiously circles the area of the sound, he will at some time show himself in the powerful rays of the light. When this occurs, the caller tempers his distress cries to a dying whimper.

If all goes well, the fox will sense an impending supper and move in somewhat closer. At this point, if the animal is within range of the hunters, the person with the light will immediately change its beam from a wide spread to a pointed ray. This he will direct at the animal's eyes or face. For a very few seconds, this sudden ray of blinding light has a paralyzing effect on the game, and it will stand immobile. This is the hunter's opportunity to shoot the animal if he wishes.

When one area has been "called," the party moves on to another, generally at least a mile away. The calling is then resumed.

28

Woodchuck

MANY GAME SPECIES have had to move before advancing civilization, migrating to more remote areas not so populated by man. One notable exception to this tendency is the woodchuck *(Marmota monax)*. When his forest home was gradually decimated, he actually moved in on the enemy who destroyed it. From foraging in the woods for his sustenance, the woodchuck turned with alacrity to feeding off the rich farm crops of the newly cultivated lands.

Woodchucks are widely distributed, ranging generally from the east coast as far west as Oklahoma. Northward, their range includes parts of Alaska. The animals are prolific in nature and hibernate during the colder ·months, generally from late September to March. Both these factors help to keep their numbers up, in spite of heavy hunting in some sections of the country. The woodchuck is highly prized by varmint hunters, who are equipped for the sport with sophisticated precision rifles. Because the species has adapted itself to living off the lush domestic crops man produces, it has had both to make its home on cultivated lands and to become most wary in nature. Few animals are wiser or harder to approach than an old woodchuck.

The woodchuck is one of the larger rodents. Adults measure nearly 2 feet in length and weigh up to 10 pounds or so. The animal is dark brown with lighter grizzled areas around the face, squat in shape, and has a sizable flattish tail.

The woodchuck's tracks are more or less round in shape, and like those of many of the hoofless quadrupeds, they show the footpad and claw and toe marks. They differ, however, from some animal tracks in that only four toes and claws of the front foot leave imprints, whereas all five toes of the rear foot are visible in the track. Both front and hind tracks measure up to 1½ inches in length.

Tracking a woodchuck is something of an inverse situation. With many animal species, the hunter finds a recent track, then trails on or parallel to it until he comes upon the animal that made it. Fresh woodchuck tracks, on the other hand, are likely to be found at or near the den where the animal probably holed up.

The woodchuck generally likes meadow and pasturelands where he can dig his burrow in the soil. Mostly, within these lands, he favors small knolls, rocky slopes, and other mild rises where he can burrow without being disturbed, and into which water will not drain or run. Because his burrow is his major protection against enemies, during the months he is out of hibernation he is never far from it. He likes to sit upright, near the burrow entrance, look for any possible enemies, then take a short trip out for his food. Once gorged with food, he moves back to the mounded dirt around the burrow entrance and again watches for enemies. The short trails the woodchuck makes as he radiates outward from the burrow in search of food often become well-beaten little paths or runways. These frequently lead to areas of clover, alfalfa, grass, and similar vegetation for which he has a liking.

The burrows are perennial in nature in that the same areas are used from year to year, though the animals do not colonize and become gregarious as ground squirrels do.

There are three basic ways of findings these burrows and locating the animals. One is to talk with the farmers in a general area suspected of having woodchuck populations, especially those farmers having large pasture and meadow acreages that are not annually disturbed by plowing. Most farmers consider the woodchuck a pest, not only because he

Woodchucks are frequently spotted sitting upright outside a burrow collecting food or watching for enemies.

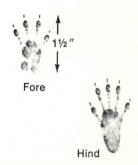

Fore

1½″

Hind

Woodchucks leave only four toes and claws in the forefoot track, while all five toes are visible in the print made by the hind foot.

It is rare to see woodchuck scat since the chuck generally buries its feces.

eats domestic crops, but because he digs holes and makes mounds which are hard on farm machinery, and into which domestic stock often fall and injure themselves. If woodchucks are in a given area, most farmers will be aware of the fact. Often they will give responsible people who will not shoot around their stock, or leave gates open, the privilege of hunting the rodents on their lands.

Another way of locating the animals is to drive about over the back roads in rolling pastureland and farm country and watch for the animals in the surrounding fields. Generally, an hour's study of the area will either show the near-black forms standing upright for a second or two or moving along the ground to and from their burrows.

Perhaps the surest way is to go into suspected woodchuck country, then study all the open pastures, knolls, slopes, and meadowlands within view with 6- to 8-power binoculars. The best time to do this is in May, when the animals are most active after hibernation, and when the young chucks are out of the burrows.

When good chuck areas are found, they may be expected to produce annually, if not depleted by too much hunting. The wise chuck hunter conserves his quarry and leaves plenty for seed. In this way he only has to find good chuck country only once.

29

Rockchuck

A WESTERN SPECIES OF RODENT comparable in most respects to the woodchuck is the rockchuck *(Marmota caligata)*. Coloration in the two species is much the same, with a trend toward lighter hues in the rockchuck. Size varies, but in general the rockchuck is the larger of the two.

The basic difference is that the eastern woodchuck likes low pasture and agricultural areas, while his western cousin likes rocky, rougher, and generally higher country. The rockchuck's range broadly coincides with the Rocky Mountains.

The rockchuck's tracks are similar to those of the woodchuck except for variations in size. There are two areas in which the tracks of this species may be found. First, in years when the snows melt early, the adult animals often emerge in late March from the rocky dens in which they have hibernated and go on short exploratory trips in search of food. These forays often take them across remaining snow patches. The tracks there, if found soon after they are made, are easily identifiable and differ from those left by magpies and other birds. Melting snows will cause them to fade rapidly, leaving only dirt specks from the earth in the chuck's den.

The second place where rockchuck tracks are left is in the immediate area of the den itself, and later in the season. The animals are never far from their dens, which offer protection against enemies. The trips they make afield are in the direction of green grasses, alfalfa fields bordering on desert country, and other foods, and seldom cover more than a few hundred feet.

Since the tracks are habitually found near the dens, which pin down the animals' permanent location, rockchucks are more often found visually than by tracking. Another form of spoor, however, is helpful in determining if the animals have emerged, or are still hibernating in the dens. This is their dung. Rockchuck dung is in segments measuring 2 inches or so in length and approximately 1/2 inch in diameter. Recent dung is medium green in color with a slimy coat. If a rocky den is being used, it is almost cer-

Rockchuck tracks often lead to the animal's permanent den.

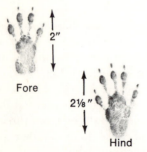

Fore

2"

2⅛"

Hind

Rockchuck tracks may be found in loose dirt near the den and in spring snows after hibernation.

Rockchuck dung is segmented and medium green in color.

tain that fresh dung will appear on top of some of the flattish rocks nearby.

The best way of finding rockchucks is to go into the type of country they like and then scout for them with high-powered glasses. The canyons formed by rivers cutting down, over the ages, through rocky terrain provide one of their favorite habitats. This is especially true in regions where agricultural crops grow on the benchlands above the rims of the gorge. Families of rockchucks will den in the upper canyon sides and make trips out into the benchland crops for food. In addition, they work the canyon sides in the grass-covered earth patches between talus slides. Two of the best areas of this type are the canyons of the Snake River and the Teton River, both in southeastern Idaho. A good way to find rockchucks in such country is to post oneself on one of the gorge rims, then set up a spotting scope and glass the opposite side of the gorge. One can pick up the moving forms of the chucks over an area of nearly a half-mile in this way, then move on to another location.

Desert country interspersed with old lava flows is another type of country rockchucks love. They den up in any of the numerous lava upthrusts, then sally forth into the surrounding sagebrush and meadow areas for grass and other vegetation. The best way to find the animals in this kind of country is to drive with a rugged four-wheel-drive vehicle over the numerous sheepherders' roads, which to a hunter are somehow negotiable; then study all lava buttes, upthrusts, and rocky hillsides with binoculars. The chucks will most often be seen as they move about over the rocks, or while sunning themselves, frequently etched against the sky, atop a high rock pile.

Morning is the best time to look for rockchucks, except on a stormy or windy day, when they tend to stay in their dens. Often on a clear, windless day, chucks may be found audibly. That is, an adult will occasionally give his high-pitched, whistling *Wheet!* call, which carries for nearly a half-mile. With practice one can learn to simulate the call with a shrill whistle, and often a chuck will answer.

Rockchucks can be found only between late March, when they generally emerge, and late August, when they normally go back into their rocky dens for winter hibernation. The same dens are very likely to be used year after year unless the chuck population is killed off.

Melanism occasionally occurs in rockchucks. A hunter seeing what he takes to be a black house cat running about on a distant rock pile had better give it a second look. It may be a jet-black rockchuck. I have seen and killed them in various areas of the West.

A northern species of the chuck family is the yellow-footed marmot *(Marmota flaviventris)*, which is quite simiar to the woodchuck and rockchuck and lives generally in Canada, Alaska, and a few scattered areas in the lower forty-eight states. This species is known colloquially as the whistling marmot, or simply the "whistler." He lives in the high rocky slopes and slides of such areas as the Cassiar Mountains, and one often sees him in early fall while hunting rams and grizzlies in the high rocky canyon heads. The whistler has the dubious distinction of being the last food the high-country grizzly eats before he too goes into hibernation.

30

Ground Squirrel

WHEREAS TREE SQUIRRELS use the forests for their homes, protection, and food supply, ground squirrels utilize the earth for these same purposes.

There are several species of ground squirrels, depending largely upon the region, but all have the same general life cycle. One of the best known of them is the prairie dog *(Cynomys ludovicianus)*. As his name suggests, this species lives in the Great Plains area, generally from the eastern edge of the Mississippi basin westward to the Rocky Mountains and southward to Mexico. Around the turn of the century, the prairie-dog population was so intense in some of the plains states that great areas of grasslands were destroyed, and the rodents threatened the existence of such agricultural crops as grain and alfalfa. A mass extermination program was instituted in some areas, and the prairie-dog populations were almost wiped out.

These various species of squirrels are known in various parts of the country as ground squirrels, sod poodles, chiselers, picket posts, and barking squirrels. This last name was given them because of their habit of running from danger to the edge of their hole, standing upright, twitching their short tails, and giving a shrill *Terk!* cry before departing down the hole.

Ground squirrels live in a network of holes radiating from a central entrance hole at the surface of the ground. Many of the side holes go down several feet. The entrance hole at the surface is mounded up, since it serves as a dumping ground for the excavated earth, and thereby helps to keep groundwater from entering the burrows. The type of light soil necessary for this kind of burrowing gives one a clue as to the possible location of the animals.

Unlike some species, the ground squirrel is gregarious in the extreme. He lives with his fellows in extensive colonies. Often the burrowing done by these colonies will damage innumerable acres of agricultural lands. In the West, vast areas of summer elk ranges are being extensively damaged.

The ground squirrel's tracks are comparable to those of small tree squirrels. The average ground squirrel measures about 14 inches in length, including a short, flattish tail that accounts for nearly a third of this length. The front track shows the imprint of only four toes and measures about 3/4 inch in length. The hind track shows the imprint of all five toes and measures a full inch in length.

This species, being one of the most diminutive and lightest of our small-game animals, leaves but a slight imprint as it moves over the ground. Occasionally a track will show in wet earth, but usually it is but a minimal disturbance of the soil. Even at the mounded entrance of the hole, the packed-down soil often shows no individual imprint. For this reason, it is impossible to track a ground squirrel beyond the recognition of but a few imprints. Moreover, there is no need to do so. As in the case of the rockchuck, when the hunter finds an identifiable track, he has already virtually located the burrow, where the animal will be.

Again like the chuck family, ground squirrels live in their labyrinthine underground dwellings and make only short surface trips, radiating from the hole in every direction, to gather prairie grass, hay, grain, and other green foods.

These little animals like open-range and prairie country that has dirt soils and a moderate rainfall. Other good places to locate them are high dirt embankments and cuttings, especially on back-country roads, the big, undisturbed banks along irrigation canals, long fence lines that are not annually tilled, and cutbanks

Ground squirrels, better known as "prairie dogs," seldom stray far away from their burrows.

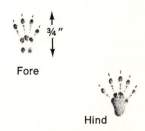

Fore

Hind

Tracks left by prairie dogs show only slight disturbance to the soil.

It is rare to see ground squirrel dung. Like the woodchuck, the ground squirrel buries its feces.

where they can dig in, and which are adjacent to grassland or crops. They also like the sandy loam soils often found in the sparse sagebrush country of the West.

When an animal is sighted, one will find the colony nearby, and the animal will probably just have run down the entrance hole. To get a further look, or the opportunity to hunt the species, it is best to move off some distance to a vantage point if possible, and then patiently wait. Usually if one moves a hundred yards or so away from a hole, the animal or animals will reappear shortly.

Years ago, I photographed several ground squirrels on our own acreage. They had established a colony in the dirt cutbank of an old riverbed. By anchoring the camera 10 feet from the entrance hole, then running 75 feet of fishing line from the shutter to where I lay partially concealed in the weeds, I could get a single picture after a half-hour wait. Each time the shutter clicked, the emerging squirrel would twitch his stubby tail, turn on a dime, and bore back down the hole.

Porcupine

ALMOST EVERY WILD-GAME SPECIES has some form of built-in protection against its enemies. This may be fleetness of foot, protective coloration, exceptional vision, or a combination of such factors. The protection that nature has given the lowly porcupine *(Erethizon dorsatus)* is a back and tailful of needlelike quills, which can be erected at will, and which deter most enemies. These quills are barbed like tiny arrowheads, and once into flesh, they continue working inward. In normal movement, the porcupine keeps these pale yellow, black-tipped quills more or less flattened to its back. But once aroused or startled, the animal raises the quills upright and is ready to defend itself with complete hedge of miniature spears.

An adult porcupine weighs up to 40 pounds and measures nearly 3 feet in length. Among the rodents of North America, it is second in size only to the beaver. It is squat in appearance, dark gray in color, nearly black along the spine, and has a medium-length, tapering tail. Its distribution is over much of Canada, some areas of the West, and in the Northeast. The species is found generally in forested areas, particularly coniferous forests.

Porcupine tracks resemble, in miniature, those made by a man or a bear, except in one respect. The pads are not arched but show the imprint of the entire foot, with toe and clawmarks set out in front. In snow the pad imprints look like those of some toy snowshoe. As with some other species, only four toe marks show in the tracks of the forefeet, whereas there are five toe marks in the hind tracks. The imprint of the front tracks measure up to 3 inches in length, while the rear ones often run to 4 inches.

This species does not hibernate, and consequently the tracks are often seen in snow. In thin snow, the tracks can be mistaken for those of a bear cub. In deep snow, the animal's short legs do not keep it off the snow, and the spoor consists of a semicircular channel pressed into the snow, with the tracks at its bottom. In either snow or bare earth, the tracks are pigeon-toed, owing to the animal's slow, waddly gait.

In most areas porcupines are not numerous enough to insure success if

Bark stripped from a coniferous tree in early spring is a sign that porcupines are within tracking range.

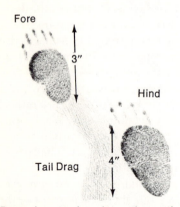

Fore

3"

Hind

Tail Drag   4"

Porcupine tracks show the entire foot. There will be four toe and claw marks showing in the print. Often, the drag mark of the tail shows between the tracks.

Porcupine scat often contains pieces of undigested bark.

one goes to look for the animal. Generally it is coincidentally located, while one is in the woods for other game or purposes. Porky loves to feed on the bark of coniferous trees. Often the first indication of the presence of a porcupine in the woods is what appears to be a dark bunch of parasitic foliage or a big magpie's nest up in the trees. A second careful look often shows this scraggly form to be a porcupine, in the process of eating tree bark. At lower elevations, one often sees a porky up a thick bunch of willows, riding their tops as they bend over. The big rodent also likes to invade outlying apple orchards, where it chews on the bark of the upper branches.

In thick spruce country, a common way to find the animal is to look for patches on the trees that it has stripped of bark. It will often stay in a thick stand of spruce trees feeding in this way for several days at a time. It may well bark the trees for a stretch of several feet along the trunks, or still more frequently it girdles them completely in places, causing death to the trees. A dozen or more trees are sometimes girdled within a 100-yard area. This habit has been responsible for the changing of the porcupine's status. Once it was considered man's friend, and at times his salvation in that it was the only forest animal that a lost man could run down, kill with a weapon no more sophisticated than a club, and eat. Currently, because of its great destructiveness in girdling live trees, it is considered a pest.

One seemingly certain way to locate a porcupine in most big wooded areas is simply to take the family dog along on forest hikes. For some reason, it will invariably find a porcupine if there is one within range. The dog comes up to the quilly animal as it waddles along the ground and, thinking that it is easy prey, approaches close enough for the porky to switch its thorny tail and fill Rover's snout with barbed little spears. These will never come out, unless pulled painfully from the dog's nose with pliers.

Another and rather questionable way of finding a porcupine is to let the animal find you. Porky has a great liking for salt, particularly for such things as ax handles, shovels, and leather saddlery impregnated with the salty perspiration of man or horse. Usually he is attracted to them at night. A personal experience will serve as illustration. In the Wind River Mountains once, when we made camp, we thought to thwart any possible porcupine incursion by stowing away all the riding and decker saddles inside a 7-foot miner-type tepee and tying the flap shut. But somehow, during the night, a wandering porky managed to get inside through the flap and generally wreck things. The leather rigging of two packsaddles was chewed up and ruined, and the stench from animal's urine and dung on the canvas floor made it necessary to destroy the tent.

PREDATORS

32

Coyote

THE PERSON WHO HAS NOT HEARD A COYOTE CRY, on a frosty morning in desert country, has missed one of the most thrilling calls of the wilderness. It is eerie, distinctive, and the essence of loneliness.

The coyote *(Canis latrans)* is about the size of a small dog, the adults weighing 35 pounds or more and measuring nearly 4 feet in length. Its coloration ranges from yellowish gray in summer to light gray in winter. Its distinguishing features are a sharp, pointed nose, slanting eyes, erect ears that never flop over like those of many dogs, and a long tail, or brush, that seems to give the animal stability when running. I once saw an adult coyote whose tail had been broken up fairly close to the junction with its body, and which could not run fast without tumbling over.

No other species, perhaps, has been more persecuted by man than the little yellow dog. Because of the inroads coyotes make into poultry and domestic stock, as well as some of the game animals, man has waged a continuing war against them. Despite this, the coyote has succeeded in living almost in man's backyard, matching wits with his enemies and maintaining his numbers and distribution. The overall range of this small desert dog is from the tree line in northern Alaska to Central America. His greatest numbers are found in the west of the continent.

The tracks of a coyote are roundish in overall contour and quite like those of a small dog. The tracks of the adult animal measure up to 2½ inches and show the imprints of four toes, their claws, and the footpad. The major difference between the front and hind tracks is in the pad imprint. The hind pad shows a small heel extension.

The tracks of this species often show in the dust of high game trails that have not been recently used by man or horse. The animal seems to like to cut in to such a trail, follow it for a short distance, then move out of it to where vegetation conceals the tracks. In moving about after elk, deer, or other high-country game, one may well spot a distant coyote moving, usually along a ridge trail. In the fall, when there is light snow on the trails,

The lonely howl of the coyote is a characteristic sound of western North America. The animal gives voice at dusk and daybreak.

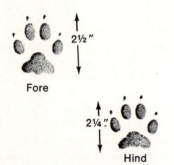

In forest and brushlands, one rarely finds coyote tracks. Its doglike imprint, however, is often evident in snow, dust or sand.

Fore — 2½"

Hind — 2¼"

The scat of the coyote resembles that of a dog and contains mostly hair.

it is possible to follow coyote tracks, made early that same day, for considerable distances. Daybreak or early morning are the best times to do this, as the animals move more than later in the day. Often a coyote can be "jumped" at a distance in this way.

In such game country, when a deer or elk is killed, coyotes normally come to the offal left after dressing the animal. Except immediately after a heavy, wet snowstorm, they usually do not touch a hung game carcass for the first 24 hours, if some kind of scare-piece is left with the game. A handkerchief, an empty shell, or even excessive handling of the meat will keep them circling a few rods away for the first day. By coming back to check hung game the first and second mornings after the kill, the hunter will often spot a coyote near it, if he approaches upwind and noiselessly.

In heavy and recent desert snows, a thrilling way to find a coyote is on horseback. The snow should be about a foot deep, fluffy, and freshly fallen that night. The hunter should trailer-haul his saddle horse to the coyote area by daybreak. The spot chosen must be extensive, have no fence lines, and have a jackrabbit population if possible. Some of the big sage-brush stands and desert areas of the West still meet these requirements.

Once into the area, the hunter mounts his horse and strikes off, watching for fresh tracks. Often he will not have to go more than a half-mile or so, especially in years of good coyote populations, before he strikes the track of a coyote, freshly made as it hunts for jackrabbits. The rider then starts trailing the animal as it moves in and out of the sagebrush. But before long the cagey yodel-dog, aware that he is being pursued, strikes off in a straight line. At this point, the rider begins to make his horse alternate between a fast trot and a gentle gallop, in order to pace it for a long but fast run. Normally, after "bucking" the heavy snow for a mile or two, the coyote will tire. The last hundred yards or so are covered at a gallop, and at this stage the coyote will wring his tail and often lie down exhausted.

The modern snowmobile has almost put an end to this exhilarating form of horseback hunting. The little snow buggies are now used in much the same manner, except that the chase is generally over more open country, and the coyote can be run down in less time.

One of the yodel-dog's main foods is the jackrabbit. Coyotes can often be located in shallow snow by driving a rugged snow-tired jeep or pickup truck over big areas of roadless desert country and watching for the gray predators as one goes along. The thicker the jackrabbits, the better chance there is of seeing a coyote in that spot. The first thing one sees is generally a pair of pointed ears or a low, gray, horizontal form in the distant sagebrush. Often where one finds one coyote in such a place, far removed from any settlement, there will be others.

Another way of locating a coyote in desert country is to watch the great golden eagle as it hunts from the air. The eagle spots a jackrabbit, dives down upon it from a height, kills it, and begins to eat. The wise little desert pup watches the eagle do this from his ground position, then follows and takes the remains from the big bird — if he can. Otherwise, in order to catch the fast jackrabbit, coyotes have to run them in relays.

The best month for any kind of desert hunting of coyotes is February. This is the mating month, when the animals tend to be grouped together and are somewhat less wary.

Ranchers in forest-cattle ranges have found a unique way to hunt coyotes. This involves going to one of their haystacks set in a meadow where coyotes come to dig for mice and other rodents. Before daybreak, they hide in the top of the haystack, using it as a blind. The unsuspecting yodel-dog moves out into the meadow from fringing timber and comes within rifle range.

Coyotes can be found incidentally when the hunter is after almost any other species of big game. This is particularly so in the case of the antelope and the rockchuck, both of which inhabit the same type of desert regions as the predator. The coyote preys heavily on young antelope. During the spring fawning season, a big dog coyote will patiently watch the distressed doe, as she moves about in one small area several hours before dropping the fawn. Once she has given birth, he will move up to the place and kill the fawn in spite of the doe. For this and other reasons, good places to watch for coyotes are the fringes of antelope bands.

Coyotes may often be approximately located by their weird little *Yip-yip-yip, yowr-r-r-oooo!* cry. Usually they are heard at dusk and daybreak, but often in wild country they howl during broad daylight. Two coyotes calling to each other across a desert basin or from two adjoining hilltops will sound like a whole chorus of the yodelers. But by listening intently, one can pick out their individual voices. It is profitable to look for coyotes in those areas where they were heard the night before, or at dawn the same day.

The laziest way to look for coyotes is, of course, to let the animals look for the hunter. This is done by calling to the animals on an artificial varmint call, in known coyote country. The caller, wearing camouflaged clothing, waits concealed in some natural blind formed by a bush or other vegetation. He then simulates the distressed call of a caught or dying rabbit, as is done when calling other species such as foxes.

33

Bobcat

THE BOBCAT OR WILDCAT *(Lynx rufus)* is another predator comparable to the coyote in size. It measures nearly 3 feet in length and can weigh up to 35 pounds, and considerably more in the case of exceptional specimens. We estimated one I killed in the Rapid River country of central Idaho at 50 pounds or slightly over. We found, upon skinning him, that he was rolling in fat from the kills that he had been able to make in a winter concentration of small deer.

The coloration of the species is an overall gray, mottled with muted black spots and barred markings. The general effect is one of camouflaging, which blends well with the forest foliage and rocks within the bobcat's habitat. His most distinguishing feature is perhaps the short tail, which earns him his name.

The distribution of the bobcat, although not as extensive as that of the coyote, is still considerable. The animal ranges from the Canadian border to Mexico in the West and from the Saint Lawrence River to the swamps of Florida in the East. This distribution does not seem to be determined by any definite terrain, elevation, or type of vegetation. Bobcats are found in a variety of habitats such as swampland, high rocky mountains, or flat agricultural lands. Like the whitetail deer, they have learned to live in man's backyard.

Bobcat tracks are unique in that the pad imprints are blurred by the hair that comes down on the feet well into the toes area. The tracks measure around 2½ inches in length, and four toes show on each foot, but without the marks of the claws. Where a track shows up well in soft earth or mud, the heel mark is more clearly defined than with many other species. Moreover, when the animal is walking, the space between sets of tracks, which measures about 6 inches, is smaller than it is in the case of many other species.

In snow, the tracks lose much of their definition, because, under the animal's weight, the hair pushes down into the track along with the pads of

A bobcat sometimes leaves claw marks like these.

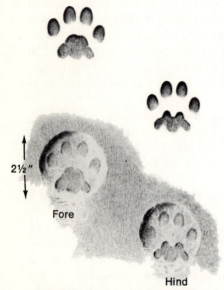

2½"

Fore

Hind

The bobcat's tracks show four toe pads on each foot with a space of 6 inches between tracks. The claws retract when the animal walks. In snow the print appears round and without much definition.

Scat of the bobcat is about ¾ inch in diameter. It usually can be distinguished from that of the dog or coyote by its covering of natural debris.

the toes and heel. The effect is as if a powder puff had been pushed down into the snow with a stick of nearly the same diameter. The imprint is nothing but a soft, deep depression.

In snow, unless other animals have cut in, it is possible to trail a bobcat for considerable distances. Except when he is pursued and knows it, the tracks will meander in and out among trees and bushes, as he hunts for such food as rodents, birds, and the young of medium-sized game animals. Normally, however, he will see anyone who trails him long before he is jumped at close range. This is due to his camouflaged coloration and to the fact that this species, like most others, watches its backtrack.

There are two basic ways of finding a bobcat. The first may seem haphazard, but for the person who hunts other game considerably, and without dogs, it yields results more often than might be expected. The technique is simply to forget about bobcats and go about hunting numerous other field species such as deer, elk, moose, bear, antelope, or other predators. By the law of averages, an observant and persistent hunter must at some time or other chance upon a bobcat.

My own experience is a good example of this. The first three bobcats I saw, in nearly a lifetime in the outdoors, appeared when I was doing something other than looking for a bobcat. One big cat appeared 35 yards away, as we hunted ducks in some marshland interspersed with small knolls of short sagebrush. No ducks had appeared for some time, and we were waiting for a flight while concealed in some tules. All of a sudden this big cat walked right out before us from the fringing tules where he had undoubtedly been hunting ducks himself. The second bobcat cut into the fresh trail of some mule deer I was tracking, after a recent snowfall. I was only a half-mile behind them (as events later proved), and the cat cut in and began following them ahead of me. I came up as he sneaked along, and his mounted pelt now tells the rest of the tale. A third bobcat materialized shortly after a pack owner had turned his hounds loose on what he thought was a small cougar track in deep winter snow. But the track turned rapidly into something else as the hounds took off baying to high heaven. Within moments, they treed a huge bobcat up a 90-foot white pine tree. He was there panting, when we came up.

The only really successful way to hunt bobcats is with dogs. Hounds that are good on foxes are fine also for coursing bobcats. Such hunting takes two forms. In swampy country or other areas where bobcats do not like to "tree," the hounds are turned loose, and the hunters post themselves on ridges, runways, and game crossings, where the pursued cat is likely to run. Suitable spots include relatively small areas of cover, in which the bobcat prefers to circle and stay, rather than break out across open spaces.

In the forested regions of the West, bobcat country often coincides with good cougar country, and the cats here will generally tree. Many hound owners prefer not to bother with bobcats when there is a chance of the big cougar. Often they spend years training their hounds not to chase bobcats and will not turn them loose, in snow, on the tracks of the smaller species. But in fall, before the first snows, they will often loose the dogs on any fresh scent where they cannot identify the tracks, in the hope that it will be a cougar. There are also some hound owners who like to chase bobcats and who have hounds for the purpose. The chase is like that for cougar, with the hunters catching up to the hounds later, at the treed animal. The Walker hound is among the very best breeds for chasing bobcats.

Like foxes and coyotes, bobcats can be called up on an artificial varmint call, an art that is fast growing popular.

34

Lynx

THE CANADIAN LYNX *(Lynx canadensis)* is another of the feline predators. And as the name suggests, the lynx has a wide distribution in Canada, and his range also extends northward into Alaska. This cat may be compared to the bobcat in general appearance and size. The lynx is tawny-gray, much the same overall color as the black-tailed jackrabbit. Adults weigh up to 40 pounds, or more in the case of exceptional specimens.

The lynx differs from the bobcat in that it has more tufted ears and a more pronounced ruff of hairs around the face. The bottom part of this ruff comes well down below the animal's face, something like two drooping sideburns. The tail of the lynx is shorter than that of the bobcat, being just an abbreviated stub. Its feet, on the other hand, are larger than those of the bobcat. As in the case of the snowshoe rabbit, on which the lynx largely survives, these oversized feet are nature's provision for moving easily over the winter snows without sinking in.

On soft summer earth, lynx tracks show four toe marks without the imprint of the claws, which is obscured by the heavy hairs of the foot. The tracks also show a triangular heel pad. An adult's tracks measure a full 3 inches across the toe pads, and the space between sets of tracks is not much longer than in the case of the bobcat, averaging 6 to 7 inches.

In winter, this animal's tracks are different and larger. Under the weight of the lynx the heavily furred feet come down in such a way that the fur also leaves an imprint in soft winter snow. The tracks are virtually round in contour, and except for their slightly broken edges, they look like the impression left in the snow by a shallow round disc. The overall winter track measures 4 inches or more.

The factors complicate tracking of this animal. First, the lynx is nocturnal in habit and, unless flushed by dogs, it spends the day hiding in deep thickets and rocky outcrops. Secondly, in its northern ranges, any tracks occurring in fresh snow, cannot usually be followed except with snowshoes because of the depth of snow. Trappers occasionally see a lynx while covering their traplines on webs or with dog teams. Occasionally they use their dogs to course one of the animals and tree it, but they take most of their lynxes by trapping them.

Because the lynx's range is normally in the remote and sparsely populated areas of the North, the animal is rarely hunted for sport. During the winter season when his pelt is prime, a lynx-hunting expedition simply involves too much hard physical effort, except for the hunter living close to lynx country. However, the recent popularity of the dependable little snowmobiles, plus a dwindling supply of other huntable game, may well change the situation somewhat. Snowmobiles now travel almost any kind of winter country, and the recent upsurge in oil exploration, by creating many wilderness trails and roads, has helped to make this feasible. It is no longer such an undertaking to take a couple of dogs on a pair of snowmobiles, make a winter trip into forested country, pick up a wandering lynx's track, and let the hounds run him up a tree. In the future, such a testing winter jaunt may well become an intriguing winter activity for the hardy sportsman. The jumping-off spots for such expeditions will largely be outlying stock ranches, trappers' cabins, outfitters' lodges, and the wilderness homes of Canadian and Alaskan residents.

The lynx is a nocturnal animal and spends the days hiding in deep thickets and rocky outcrops.

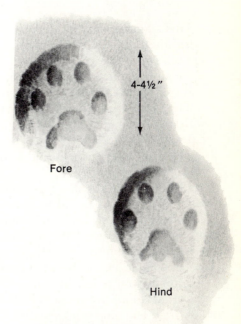

Fore

4-4½″

Hind

Lynx tracks look nearly round as the animal's fur leaves an imprint of 4 inches or more in snow.

In cat fashion, the lynx normally covers its scat.

35

Skunk

THERE ARE SEVERAL SUBSPECIES OF SKUNKS, of which the common skunk *(Mephitis mephitis)* is characteristic. Like all the species, this small animal has the self-protective capacity to throw a spray of liquid from its anal vent upon any pursuer or tormentor at close range. This spray is foul-smelling and can also cause temporary blindness.

The skunk is a squat little animal, generally striped black and white, or with stripes mingled with spots. It is further characterized by a long, bushy tail and a slow, waddly gait. The front feet have long claws, which the animal uses in digging. Adult skunks weigh up to 8 pounds and measure up to 24 inches in length.

Distribution of the skunk generally extends over most of the lower forty-eight states, Canada, and southern Alaska. In some regions the skunk is considered a purely fur-bearing animal, but in most places it is regarded as a predator because of the inroads it can make into the nests, eggs, and young of game birds, as well as into domestic poultry.

The hind tracks of the adult skunk look something like a miniature version of the tracks left by a man's foot. The entire pad of the hind foot shows, as do all five toes. The claw marks of the hind feet seldom show, however. The hind track measures up to 2½ inches in overall length. The front tracks are just over half that length, but instead of being elongated, they are roundish in appearance. They too show the marks of all five toes, as well as the five claw marks set well out in front.

When the skunk is running, the front imprints fall inside the hind ones, as if the animal were throwing earth back between his hind feet with his forepaws. In walking, the forefeet are more widely separated and leave tracks that generally coincide with those of the hind feet.

Unless one wants the animal for its pelt or a close-up picture, the only motive for locating a skunk must be the desire to remain far away from its vicinity. The ways of locating the animal are generally based upon its wanderings in quest of food. It likes brushy country and wastelands, high weeds in unplowed fields, woodlots, wild-rose patches, long willow banks, and river-bottom lands adjoining open agricultural fields. In such brushy areas it can find insects, mice, and the otherwise protected nests of game birds.

Early and late in the day, skunks often emerge from their brushy homes and wander out along the edges of open hayfields and pasturelands. Their tracks in any dusty trails skirting such places will show their presence, even if one does not catch sight of the animals themselves. A dog, however, will usually find a skunk in adjacent brush.

The species likes to dig holes in dry, unmolested areas, for example under abandoned farms and buildings that are adjacent to brushlands where the skunks work. Even on inhabited farms in outlying rural areas, skunks may dig holes under some of the seldom-used buildings before they are detected.

Skunks sometimes settle in growing crop fields such as grain and alfalfa and are not discovered until harvest. Often a farmer mowing a last swath of hay will push a skunk from before his cutter bar. Consequently a good place to watch out for a skunk is in the final stands of crops during harvesting.

Farmers living adjacent to brushlands often have their poultry houses raided by skunks. The animal usually comes between dusk and daylight. Once he has successfully stolen domestic chickens, he will return until he has been killed.

Beekeepers who keep their hives in patches of wasteland within agricultural crops also suffer from the skunk's depredations. The animal

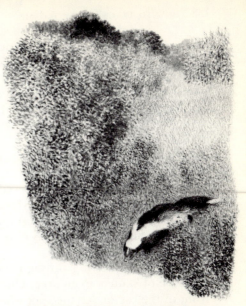

Skunks inhabit most of North America. Nocturnal animals, they are omnivorous, feeding on mice, eggs, insects, grubs, berries, garbage.

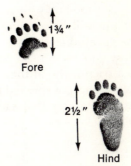

The forefoot tracks of the skunk are rounded, while the hind-foot tracks are elongated.

Skunk droppings may vary in appearance depending on the animal's diet. Diameters may reach ⅝ inch.

loves honeybees and will come, generally at dusk, in quest of them. He has a clever, instinctive way of getting at the bees in a hive that he cannot tip over. He scratches at the sides of the hive until the bees inside get agitated. Then, when they begin to appear at the entrance, he moves so that his brushy tail is near that spot. When the enraged bees get onto his tail, sometimes in a ball of moving insects, the skunk moves away from the hive, picks them off, and eats them.

In some of the most rural areas, and especially in years when mice are in short supply, skunks often come right into farmyards and climb into garbage cans in search of food, especially meat scraps. Only last fall when my next-door neighbor went at daybreak to her burning-barrel to toss in the garbage, she dumped it right on top of a skunk in the barrel. Both came out flying. She thought it was only the neighbor's black tomcat until the odor hit her.

Often simply driving through the countryside at night will reveal the presence of skunks in an area. One may see the animal cross the road in front of the car or see the spot where a skunk has been hit and killed by another car.

Anyone moving through very thick brush should do so cautiously, for this is where skunks are most apt to be during the day. When one is sprayed by a skunk, it takes strong measures to counteract the stench left on the clothes and person. Repeated washing with strong soap and water will remove most of the smell, as will soaking the clothes in tomato juice. If the clothing is too bulky, or not worth the tomato juice, burying it in soft earth overnight will help remove the odor. Often the wisest way to deal with skunk-sprayed clothing is simply to throw it away or burn it.

Close, violent contact with a skunk often leaves powerful memories. I have a friend who at the age of fourteen dug a skunk out from under an old barn, and got sprayed full in the face. Now, as an old man, he tells me, "You know, after that sad affair, I never could get so I could eat fried onions."

Finding Downed or Wounded Game

Up till now the matter of finding and tracking live game has been considered. It is equally important, if not more so, to be able to track and locate game that has been downed or wounded by the hunter. Such game, if not recovered, will be wasted.

The first step in finding downed game is to mark down the spot where the game dropped or was last seen. This can be done, even at extended shooting distances, by making a mental note of the spot's relationship to some object or natural feature such as a nearby tree, rock bluff, or distinctive bush. Even in comparatively flat or bare country, there is always some dip in elevation, some kind of vegetation or change in the color of the terrain that can serve as a point of reference.

The next step is to mark the spot from which the hunter shot, so that if an initial search for the game proves fruitless, he can return to this spot and try again. The position can be marked by tying a handkerchief to a high bush or tree limb, where he can see it from a distance.

Once these two points have been established, the hunter must estimate the distance from where he stands to the dropped game. With short distances, this is relatively easy. It becomes more difficult and more vital at long ranges such as 300 or 400 yards. Estimating ranges also becomes more difficult if it involves complex terrain and vegetation.

In order to estimate long ranges accurately, one should base the estimate on multiples of a known distance. If one walks 100 yards to work, or can throw a rock 50 yards, or has a radish patch that is 30 yards from an apple tree, such a known factor can be used as the basis for the estimate. One simply thinks, "That deer dropped just about three times as far as I walk to work, or maybe six times as far as I can throw a rock." The distance is then approximately 300 yards.

With the game marked down in relation to some landmark, the hunter's position also marked, and the distance between them estimated, the next step is carefully to pace off this intervening distance, while keeping one's eye always on the spot where the game apparently went down. Often the hunter has to deviate from his course because of intervening trees, rocky bluffs, or lake edges. He must carefully compensate for such deviations by going an equal number of paces in the opposite direction after skirting the obstacle. Moreover, such detours mean that he must increase the original distance estimate. As he goes around obstacles, he should continue to pace off this original distance mentally.

If all this is done with care, and if the game died where it fell, ninety times out of a hundred the hunter will come either directly upon it or close enough to spot it as he looks around him. In heavy brush or any kind of high foliage, he should make a close scrutiny of everything in the immediate area, since the animal's protective coloration will make it hard to see.

If the game is not spotted at this point, the next step is to mark that particular place with a coat, shirt, or other object placed as high on foliage as possible, so that it can readily be seen. This marker is then used as the center of widening concentric circles that are described, about 3 to 5 yards apart, all around it. While moving about in these progressively larger circles, the hunter should scrutinize everything within view, especially between himself and the circle's center.

These circles should progress until the game has been spotted. If, however, the game was not dead or nearly dead when it dropped, it will have moved away from the spot, leaving numerous tracks. Here is where the skill of the tracker comes into play. He starts all over again from the marker, but this time, when making the concentric circles, he looks not for game but for tracks. At this stage, another factor enters. If the game is only wounded, it will normally head either downhill, or for the heaviest cover, or both. The circles should be described all the way around the center spot, but the tracker should concentrate on those places which run downhill or lead to heavy cover. He should look not only for definite tracks but also for such things as a freshly turned leaf, stick, or bit of earth that indicate an animal's hurried passage. The tracks may be widely separated, as the wounded animal will move as fast as possible.

Locating downed game. From A, the hunter shoots the animal at B. Next, he marks B mentally by noting its relationship to a feature such as a tree or rock. He then marks A by tying a handkerchief to a bush or tree that will be visible from B. (This will help the hunter maintain his sense of direction and allow him to return to reassess the terrain if necessary.) At B, he marks the spot with clothing or pack and searches in a pattern of expanding concentric circles, covering the area thoroughly. This procedure should yield either the game or sign. If it's sign and they temporarily play out along the escape route, the hunter should again search in concentric circles until picking up the route. He repeats this process until he either jumps the game or locates it down. (Badly-wounded game often heads downhill or for heavy cover.)

Once a definite track is located, the hunter should leave his marker in the new spot and begin to trail the animal from there. This is done, as explained earlier, by carefully unraveling the trail, going meticulously from track to track. If this is painstakingly done, either the hunter will come upon his game, or he will come to a place where he can no longer find a succeeding track. In the second case, he again marks the position of the last track plainly, so that he can return and try again if necessary, and again makes concentric circles around the spot, beginning at the center. If he uses as much care as before, he will at some time, as he makes these circles, come upon another track. He then trails again, until he finds the animal or again loses the tracks. In the latter case he again marks the last track and proceeds to circle once more. The process is repeated until the game is ultimately found.

As it gradually weakens, wounded game lies down with increasing frequency. Since the meticulous tracking procedure outlined above takes an appreciable time, the animal will have time to stiffen up. If, as the hunter methodically tracks down the game, he also remains on the alert for a sight of the game ahead, he will eventually come upon the animal, either dead or trying to struggle away. This will give him a chance to finish it off if necessary.

Where this method of finding downed game is meticulously followed, the animal is habitually found, and there is very little loss of game.

An elk's escape route. From point A on the opposite page, the author shot a bull elk at B. The elk headed down the mountainside into heavy timber. Noticing the author in pursuit, the elk then took up an elusive course. When that failed, the elk angled into the lake at C, as shown. Then he turned abruptly and waded in shallow water for 200 yards. He reentered the timber at D and collapsed at E. The author located the reentry point by searching for sign all along the shoreline (solid line with arrows).

Index